Postsecondary Leaders' Thoughts on Diversity and Inclusion

Studies in Criticality

Shirley R. Steinberg

General Editor

Vol. 539

Maroro Zinyemba

Postsecondary Leaders' Thoughts on Diversity and Inclusion

Now What?

PETER LANG
Lausanne • Berlin • Bruxelles • Chennai • New York • Oxford

Library of Congress Cataloging-in-Publication Control Number: 2023004306

Bibliographic information published by the **Deutsche Nationalbibliothek.**
The German National Library lists this publication in the German
National Bibliography; detailed bibliographic data is available
on the Internet at http://dnb.d-nb.de.

Cover design by Peter Lang Group AG

ISSN 1058-1634
ISBN 978-1-4331-9691-1 (hardcover)
ISBN 978-1-4331-9690-4 (paperback)
ISBN 978-1-4331-9606-5 (ebook pdf)
ISBN 978-1-4331-9607-2 (epub)
DOI 10.3726/b20657

Dedication

To Tumwa, Tipa, Taka, Mudi, Taku, Chiko, Bella, Shona, Savannah, Seli, Diwa, Tanaka, Kiki, Lyka and those yet to be born: It is my hope that you, my children, nieces, and nephews will pursue postsecondary learning in a context where postsecondary leaders attend to social justice concerns in ways matter for equity. It is for your future learning experiences that I undertook this journey.

CONTENTS

LIST OF ILLUSTRATIONS

PREFACE

Since becoming a leader, I have longed for a book that discusses how leaders of postsecondary institutions who have made public commitments to values of diversity and inclusivity make meaning of these values. This is particularly important at a time when there is increasing diversity in the student population on postsecondary campuses. It is also key to understand how leaders make sense of and enact these values at a time when there are increased calls to address social justice concerns such as racism in educational contexts.

In my early years as a postsecondary leader, it quickly became apparent to me that the ways in which diversity and inclusivity were understood and enacted by postsecondary leaders did not always resonate with my positioning on these concepts. I am a black, female, African Canadian educator, and postsecondary leader. I have often been the only person of color sitting at leadership tables, a space in which I have had to mark my arrival.

As I sat at this table in my early years, I reflected on the meaning of diversity and inclusivity to postsecondary leaders. I began to question how it came to be that there were not more leaders who are Black, Indigenous, and People of Colour (BIPOC) like me. I wondered how it came to be that senior and executive leadership lacked racial diversity, despite the public commitments to diversity, inclusivity, and equity. I wondered what other dimensions of diversity were not represented at senior leadership levels. I began to question how my colleagues and leaders from other postsecondary institutions understood diversity and inclusivity. I wondered what their realities were with respect to these concepts.

Pursuing a doctoral degree was a goal I had set for myself and a natural progression in my educational journey. When the time came for me to pursue my doctoral studies, I decided to research how leaders of postsecondary institutions who have made public commitments to values of diversity and inclusivity make meaning of these values. The research study was timely given the context of increased diversity in student demographics, and the national dialogues and lectures that were taking place on racism, anti-racism, and inclusivity in the academy.

What I learned through my interactions with the postsecondary leaders who participated in my research study and from the work of fellow researchers in this field led to the development of the integrated social justice leadership framework for inclusivity. This framework signals the importance of leaders understanding themselves, their leadership practice, and the context in which they lead with a view to equity, anti-racism, and decolonization in educational contexts.

ACKNOWLEDGMENTS

I would like to acknowledge and thank Dr. Marlon Simmons, Dr. Brenda Spencer, Dr. Collen Kawalilak, and Dr. Ann Lopez for providing me with the guidance and support that was vital for research I undertook. Their feedback, comments, and thought-provoking questions allowed me to reflect on my work in ways that helped me grow as a researcher and leader.

My sincere appreciation goes to Dr. Marlon Simmons, my doctoral supervisor, for walking the doctoral journey with me the result of which is this publication. Dr. Simmons continuously challenged me to explore concepts further and reflect more deeply on my understanding of my study and the world of leadership and research

There is a common saying that a journey of a thousand miles begins with one step. I would like to thank Dr. Alice Zinyemba and Dr. Ranga Zinyemba, my parents, for encouraging me to take that first step and for mentoring me throughout this journey. Their work ethic, passion for education, and confidence inspired me.

Finally, I would like to acknowledge the unwavering support of my family, particularly Kevin, Tumwa, Tipa, and Taka, without whom this journey would not have been possible.

LIST OF ABBREVIATIONS

BC	British Columbia
BIPOC	Black, Indigenous and People of Color
EAL	English as an Additional Language
EDI	Equity, Diversity and Inclusion
LGBTQ	Lesbian, Gay, Bisexual, Transgender, Queer or Questioning
NDP	New Democratic Party
STEM	Science, Technology, Engineering and Mathematics
UCP	United Conservative Party
URM	Underrepresented Minority
UNESCO	United Nations Educational, Scientific and Cultural Organization

· 1 ·

INTRODUCTION: CURRENT REALITIES FOR LEADERS IN POSTSECONDARY CONTEXTS

How is it that public statements of commitment to diversity and inclusion are made by postsecondary leaders in response to allegations of racism? How is it that senior leadership in Canadian postsecondary institutions today lacks diversity? What do the concepts of diversity and inclusion mean to postsecondary leaders and how are they enacted? These are some of the questions that I asked myself as I tried to understand my world as a black, female, African Canadian educator, and postsecondary leader.

I have learned that my roles are complex in their own ways as they each require an acknowledgment and a negotiation of meaning and multiple realities. I began my career in postsecondary education over 15 years ago as an English as an Additional Language (EAL) instructor working with adult language learners from diverse backgrounds. Key to my role were my experiences of growing up in Zimbabwe, learning a third language, and living and working in three continents before settling in Alberta. This foundation has enabled me to recognize and appreciate the importance of diversity, inclusion, and social justice in relation to how people live, work, and learn.

As a postsecondary leader, I recognize that I am in a relative position of power and privilege within the institution at which I am employed. I have served in various leadership positions for the last decade. My postsecondary leadership journey began as an associate chair. When a chair position opened up, I applied and was the successful candidate. I then sought and achieved a position as associate dean for a faculty that has a number of programs that are attractive to international, Indigenous, and immigrant learners. I currently serve as a dean of a large faculty that attends to the educational needs of learners from a variety of backgrounds and that offers foundational and postsecondary programs. As dean, I am a member of the senior academic leadership team, and I participate in significant conversations and decision-making pertaining to institutional strategies and operations.

I also recognize that by virtue of holding a senior leadership position I am relatively privileged in terms of class. My current employment status affords me the financial benefits that many black women in Canada do not have. I grew up in a middle-class family in Zimbabwe, and I recognize that this enabled my siblings and me to enrol and learn in predominantly white and highly rated private schools, a legacy of British colonialism. Tuition at these school was affordable for very few black families. My parents, both academics, were political activists in the country's struggle for independence from the white-minority Rhodesian government. They were able to achieve their academic status and the accompanying financial benefits in postindependence Zimbabwe in part due to the sacrifices that their older siblings made under colonial rule.

Though I have relative power and privilege, I also experience the reality and disadvantages of being the only black member of the senior academic leadership team at my institution. I operate within an organizational culture and structures that are reflective of white, Western European, male, and heteronormative epistemologies. I serve as a leader in a context where diversity and inclusivity are values that are promoted. I am present at the leadership table where discussions and decisions, which are sometimes in dissonance with my own experiences and values about diversity and inclusivity, take place. Given my identity, sociohistorical background, and professional experience, I began to question how it came to be that there were not more people like me in senior and executive leadership positions. I wondered why senior leadership was not representative of the student demographic on campus. I questioned the extent to which a largely homogenous senior leadership could truly attend to the social justice concerns of the diverse student demographic. I began to question how my colleagues and leaders from other postsecondary institutions understood diversity and inclusivity. I wondered what their realities were with respect to these concepts. How do postsecondary leaders make meaning of diversity and inclusivity? I decided to find out through a research study.

My rationale for conducting this research study arose from a need to understand how leaders of postsecondary institutions in Alberta make meaning of diversity and inclusivity in educational settings. In other words, I sought to gain knowledge on how postsecondary leaders understand, interpret, and enact diversity and inclusivity in postsecondary educational settings. This came in a context of increasing diversity in the student population as a result of immigration initiatives, international education strategies, and social justice movements calling for the address of social justice issues. At the time I conducted my study, there was a paucity of research on how leaders of Albertan postsecondary institutions that have publicly stated a commitment to values of diversity and inclusion make meaning of these concepts. It is my hope that the knowledge generated from my study will inform leadership practice and succession planning to meet the demands and needs of an increasingly diverse student population.

Background and Context

Diversity and inclusion have been listed as values to which various organizations, including postsecondary institutions, commit themselves (Ahmed, 2012; Burke, 2013; DeLuca, 2013; Elam & Brown, 2005; James, 2011a; Lopez, 2016). In the last decade, there has been increased advocacy for equal rights and inclusion of historically marginalized people in North American society. Social justice movements such as #MeToo, #BlackLivesMatter, Students4Change, the LGBTQ movement, and the Truth and Reconciliation Commission Calls to Action are some examples of the increased awareness and need to address the issues of human rights and marginalization in Canadian society. Recent protests led by social justice movements have brought to the forefront issues that demand responses, action, and a reconsideration of diversity, inclusion, social justice, and equity (Lopez, 2020). For example, in the wake of protests following a racial profiling incident in a Starbucks store in 2018, Starbucks locations in Canada and the United States closed operations for a day to enable employees to attend diversity training interventions. The death of George Floyd, a black man at the hands of police in 2020, reignited the Black Lives Matter calls for an end to racism in Canada and in the United States. In solidarity, some postsecondary professors in Canada participated in a two-day protest, Scholar Strike, to draw attention to the social injustice issues faced by black, Indigenous, and people of colour (BIPOC) in academia and in society at large. Postsecondary students and high school students across Canada also engaged in protests demanding that racism in the education system be addressed. In response to the brutal death of Floyd, the Black Lives Matter protests, the Scholar Strike, and student protests that took place throughout Canada, some leaders of Canadian postsecondary institutions issued statements expressing their concern for social justice, and they restated their commitment to diversity and inclusion. I found the statements by postsecondary leaders intriguing in that they reiterated their commitments to diversity and inclusion but did not address issues of race and racism. This led me to wonder how diversity and inclusion are conceptualized by postsecondary leaders.

There is increased awareness and consciousness of social injustices, racism, and various forms of oppression in society today (Lopez, 2020). These social injustices are reflected in educational institutions. Dei and Asgharzadeh (2017) stated that "social issues, problems and concerns in the larger society are closely mirrored in schools and universities" (p. 24). The calls made in Canada by the professors who participated in the Scholar Strike and the students leading protests pointed to the need to attend to antiracism in educational settings. Dei (2014) took up antiracism education as "an action-oriented educational practice to address racism and the interstices of difference (such as gender, ethnicity, class, sexuality, ability, language, and religion) in the educational system" (p. 240). Following the protests and calls to action, there has been increased attention to how leaders in postsecondary institutions attend to calls for social justice, especially given the growing diversity in the student demographic. Educators need to respond to demographic changes (Lopez, 2020).

Increased immigration contributes to the diversity of Canada's population. Scholars, statisticians, and immigration strategists predict that the number of foreign-born individuals settling in Canada will continue to increase, and the children and grandchildren of foreign-born individuals will soon make up the majority of the Canadian population (Edmonston, 2016; El-Assal, 2018; Lopez & Olan, 2018; Statistics Canada, 2016). According to the Conference Board of Canada (El-Assal, 2018), an increase in immigration to Canada will have labour market and economic benefits for the country. Canada has an international education strategy (Foreign Affairs, Trade and Development Canada, 2014) that is designed to attract an increasing number of international students, and international students contribute to the Canadian labour market and economy (Immigration, Refugees and Citizenship Canada, 2018). Through federal and provincial programs such the Provincial Nominee Program, international students are provided with opportunities to transition to a permanent resident status and eventually Canadian citizenship status, thus allowing them to live and work the country after completing their studies. Canada's international education strategy and immigration programs contribute to the diversity of student populations in Canada's postsecondary institutions.

Similar to the situation in many countries in the Organisation for Economic Co-operation and Development, public funding for postsecondary institutions in Canada has been in decline for decades (Byron, 2002). Moreover, the decline in public funding has pushed leaders of postsecondary institutions to access funding from alternate sources, such as international education. International students in postsecondary institutions are viewed by administrators as a source of revenue in that international students are charged more tuition fees than domestic students (Eastman, 2006). This view has resulted in some postsecondary leaders developing an increasingly entrepreneurial focus characterized by business plans and international strategies (Burnett & Huisman, 2010) in order to be competitive and attract international students. The political discourse focuses on international students as an alternate revenue stream for postsecondary institutions. This contributes to the diversity of the student population on postsecondary campuses in Canada and reflects the context in which postsecondary leaders operate.

Some postsecondary leaders have stated through their institutional vision and mission statements that they recognize the importance of diversity and the need to be inclusive of diverse communities in order to meet the teaching and learning needs of all students. To this end, they have articulated diversity and inclusivity strategies and plans to meet the varying needs of diverse student populations (Burke, 2013; Hughes, 2015). Declaring commitments to diversity and inclusion calls for a questioning of "equity and power sharing within a social context that sees Whiteness as the norm" (Dei, 2000, p. 27). According to Dei (2000), a claim of commitment to diversity alone is superficial. He concurred with hooks (1992, as cited in Dei, 2000), who stated that "issues of race and racism are continually replaced with 'evocations of pluralism and diversity.' 'Anti-racism' is replaced with 'managing diversity' in many institutional settings" (p. 27).

Critical race and social justice scholars Carl E. James (2011b) and Malinda Smith (2017, 2019) have argued that despite Canada's Employment

Equity Act and decades of employment equity strategies and diversity planning, senior leaders in Canadian postsecondary institutions "remain overwhelmingly white and largely male" (Smith, 2019, para. 1). The composition of postsecondary leadership today does not reflect the increasing diversity in the student population attending these institutions (Jeffcoat & Piland, 2012), nor is it reflective of the increasing social diversity in Canada (Smith, 2017). Although gender representation in postsecondary leadership remains unequal, female representation has increased over the past few decades (Amey et al., 2002; Smith, 2017). The same cannot, however, be said of "visible minority" communities found on postsecondary campuses.

With the increasing diversity in the student population, educators need support in developing or enhancing the skills and competencies required to meet the teaching and learning needs of students in their classes (Lopez & Olan, 2019), and it falls on educational leaders to provide this institutional support. There is a need to plan for diverse leadership to "guide institutions through transformational periods of increasingly multifaceted populations that will shift campus culture for years to come" (Harvey, 2011, as cited in Wolfe & Dilworth, 2015, p. 686). Given the current postsecondary context where leaders are called to attend to social justice issues such as racism and the needs of a changing student demographic, it has become increasingly important for educational leaders to "have an understanding of diverse students' needs and how to address those needs and use that knowledge to develop the teachers' capacity and help them understand how to better meet the needs of all students" (Oliveras-Ortiz & Jones, 2016, p. 1). Furthermore, Wolfe and Dilworth (2015) also argued that there is a

> need for institutions to reexamine the culture in which their leadership and traditions have been structured in an attempt to make the campus more inclusive for the multicultural generations of today and tomorrow. If higher education is to thrive in a changing environment, the obligations of diversity and leadership must be met. (p. 685)

Education and educators play an important role in addressing social justice issues (Lopez & Olan, 2019). The education system "has the potential to maintain and reproduce the status quo that exists in the larger society. It also has the potential to challenge the dominant order … and help bring about more equitable and just living conditions for all" (Dei & Asgharzadeh, 2017, p. 25). Attending to the shifting campus culture in the postsecondary contexts calls for an inquiry into how leaders come to know of and give meaning to the concepts of diversity and inclusivity to which they state they are committed.

The demographic shifts occurring in the Canadian population due to increased immigration, focus on growing international student populations on campuses across the country, and calls to attend to social justice issues have implications for leaders of postsecondary institutions who are tasked with providing educational programming and learning experiences that meet the needs of the diverse student population. Scholars such as Burke (2013) have proposed diversity planning as a strategy for institutions to meet the needs of diverse students. Such planning requires an understanding of how leaders of institutions give meaning to diversity and how postsecondary leaders experience diversity and inclusive education.

Situating the Study

I engaged a qualitative descriptive case study with nine leaders from three postsecondary institutions in Alberta to understand how they make meaning of diversity and inclusivity. During 1-hour semistructured interviews that I conducted, leaders shared their perspectives on and experiences of diversity and inclusivity. They reflected on images they had brought with them that depicted how they perceived diversity and inclusivity in postsecondary settings. In some instances, leaders shared documents such as strategic plans with me.

As a black leader in a postsecondary educational setting, I identified four assumptions as I began this research. The first assumption was that leadership impacts educational outcomes (Lopez, 2021; Walker & Riordan, 2010). The second assumption was that diversity in leadership benefits higher education in that learning becomes more accessible and teaching methods become more inclusive of diverse learner needs (Lopez, 2016; Walker & Riordan, 2010; Wolfe & Dilworth, 2015). The third assumption was that leaders help shape meaning in and the culture of their organizations (Northouse, 2016; Zembylas & Iasonos, 2010). Finally, the fourth assumption was that the culture in which leaders operate influences their leadership practices (Burke, 2013; Dimmock & Walker, 2005).

As I began my study, I was keenly aware of my positionality. I recognized that I came to my study with an intersecting identity as both an insider and an outsider. In navigating the knowledge generation process, I acknowledged my assumptions and attended to those in my reflexive journal. I anchored the knowledge generation process in a social constructivist perspective, which allowed me to learn from the stories of other postsecondary leaders. A social constructivist perspective meant that I acknowledged that how the participants in my study made meaning of diversity and inclusivity was just as credible as any other way of making meaning (Crotty, 1998).

The three Albertan postsecondary institutions involved in the study were located in the province's two major cities: Edmonton and Calgary. The institutions varied in terms of the number of students served and the range of programming offered. That being said, the leaders of all three institutions spoke to diversity in the student, faculty, and staff population with regard to race, gender, and sexual orientation.

Each of the three institutions' websites described the institutional vision and mission. The websites also described commitments to values of diversity and inclusivity. Only one institution included a commitment to equity in addition to diversity and inclusivity. All the participants appeared to be well versed in their institutional vision, mission, and diversity and inclusivity statements.

Leader Profiles

As I mentioned earlier, nine leaders from postsecondary institutions in Alberta participated in my research study. Of the nine participants, two identified as male and seven identified as female. The two male leaders identified as persons of colour (one black and one brown) and one female leader also identified as a person of colour (brown). There were six female leaders who identified as being white. All nine participants had been in their current leadership positions for at least 1 year. The participants held various leadership roles; there were two program chairs, one program manager, one department director, two associate deans, one associate dean, one dean, and one vice-president. Participants worked in teaching and learning faculties, student life, and external relations. I would like to introduce you, the reader, to these nine leaders by providing you with some background information pertaining to each participant's leadership role, how long they had been in a leadership role, and each participant's definition of diversity and inclusivity in their own words and in relation to the artifacts they shared. With each profile, I include my observations from my field notes and reflections from my reflexive journal.

Michelle. The first leader I met with was Michelle, a program chair over-seeing foundational programs. Michelle identified as a white female. I met with Michelle in her workplace office. From what I observed making my way to her office, the institution she worked at had considerable student diversity in terms of racial and religious backgrounds. Michelle welcomed me to her office. To me, Michelle appeared to be somewhat nervous at the beginning of the interview. This is something I expected would happen as I prepared for the interviews. To help ease what I sensed to be nervousness, I began the interview with a conversation about the freezing temperatures that day. I also shared some information about myself with regard to my research interests and my role as a leader of a postsecondary institution. At the time of the inter-view, Michelle had been in leadership roles for at least 5 years. She informed me that in her current role as program chair, she managed two programs in her institution. As a program chair, Michelle described how she worked directly with instructors and supported them in delivering quality education. She also mentioned that she worked directly with students given that she teaches some courses.

For Michelle, diversity is "the recognition that people come from a vari-ety of backgrounds, experiences, and norms, and inclusivity is the effort to appreciate those differences and find commonalities and value in others." To illustrate what diversity and inclusivity in postsecondary meant to her, Michelle shared an image of travellers in an airport. For her, this image showed "that people have a common purpose. They are all travelling but they are going in different directions and they are coming from different places." When Michelle described her image to me, I learned that she drew on what the travellers had in common. The travellers symbolized the students at the institution who, like the travellers, had a common goal, the students' com-mon goal being education. They were having what Michelle called a "group experience" of finding their gate and making the plane on time. Though they also had individual experiences, at the end of the day they needed to make the flight on time. Michelle's role as a leader was to support the instructors in providing the students the necessary skills to reach their travel destinations.

Stella. The second leader I met with was Stella, an associate dean special-izing in research and innovation. Stella identified as a white female. My con-versation with Stella took place in a coffee shop away from campus. At first, I was concerned about the noise level in the coffee shop but given that we were seated in a corner far from the entrance and service desk, the noise was min-imized. Stella appeared to be very comfortable throughout our conversation.

She shared that she had recently completed her doctoral studies and could empathize with me as I was on my journey. The relaxed atmosphere in the coffee shop lent itself well to our conversation over coffee.

Stella shared that she had held a number of leadership positions in her institution. In her current role as an associate dean, she has interacted with other senior leaders at the institution as well as external stakeholders. Stella stated that "diversity to me in any sort of setting and especially the setting I work within in postsec would be diverse perspectives, diverse experiences, diverse lived experiences, diverse ways of being, knowing, and doing, diverse perspectives on knowledge systems." In previous leadership roles, Stella oversaw curriculum development projects related to the institution's Indigenization strategy. She also completed graduate studies that included a focus on Indigenous knowledge systems. Diversity and inclusivity were, so to speak, down her lane indeed.

Stella shared an image of a tree trunk with exposed roots as a metaphor of her conceptualization of diversity and inclusivity in postsecondary settings. Stella stated that the image served to show that we are no longer in a world where there are, the development of, or the containment of isolated perspectives on how we are in the world and what reality is and you know. I think that we have now gotten to a point in human history where we are all tangled. And we are all tangled together.

Orla. The third leader was Orla, an associate dean. I met with Orla in her workplace office. Orla identified as a white female. It appeared to me that Orla was guarded in her responses at the beginning of the interview. However, this changed during the interview. She had a lot of pauses and hesitations, which I attributed to the need to think and formulate her responses. It seemed as though she was processing her thoughts and really thinking carefully about what she shared. I noticed that she was wearing an LGBTQ pride lanyard. I immediately assumed that she was actively engaged in the LGBTQ community. After noticing the lanyard and the assumption I had made, I had to remind myself to put that assumption on hold and let the conversation evolve. Interestingly, Orla made reference to the colour of my skin during the conversation. This was something I didn't expect. I interpreted this as a level of awareness that Orla has of issues pertaining to diversity and inclusivity.

Orla mentioned that she had been in other leadership positions over the years. As an associate dean, she supported program chairs and faculty members in meeting the goals of the institution's strategic plan. Orla shared with me the institution's handbill outlining the strategic plan. During the conversation she brought to my attention the statements in the strategic plan that resonated with her. For Orla, diversity and inclusivity mean "how we are all different based on various factors like gender, sexual orientation, race, country of origin, socioeconomic, class… and inclusivity is how do we make sure that everybody is to count and participate and have an equal shot at things." To support this conceptualization, she drew an image of a striped person as her artifact. She stated that the image was inspired by the rainbow flag.

Kelli. The fourth leader was Kelli, a dean of a health and community studies faculty. Kelli identified as a white female. The conversation with Kelli took place in her workplace office. From the beginning of our interaction in setting up the interview and at the beginning of the interview, I was acutely aware of the positional power differential between us. This was the first interview I had conducted with a person in a higher-level position than my own. I went into the interview expecting her to be guarded in her responses. I was pleasantly surprised to find her very approachable and open to conversation. I had to remind myself that, though she was in a position of power, she had responded to the recruitment call so she could share how she, as a leader, made meaning of diversity and inclusivity. My role was to let that conversation take place and let her tell her story.

Kelli shared that she reported directly to the vice president academic. Kelli has a number of associate deans reporting to her. In her role, she supports the associate deans in meeting institutional goals and student learning needs. I got a sense from our conversation that in her role as dean, Kelli may be removed from the day-to-day operational matters pertaining to diversity and inclusivity, and that the program chairs had more engagement with these matters. For Kelli, diversity and inclusivity mean "adjusting your personal context to the place that you are, the people that you are with and understanding how they are or function. It's really about being aware of your surroundings and who you're engaging with to ensure that the context that we're in or the surroundings that we're in and beyond engage with everyone in one way or another."

To share what diversity and inclusivity mean to her in a postsecondary context, Kelli presented a collage of nine pictures. The first picture portrayed faculty and staff members from different departments sitting together at lunch time in a room. Kelli mentioned that in this group was one female Indigenous faculty member. The second picture showed students of diverse racial backgrounds in the hallways of the institution. The third picture was of a bulletin board with information on events and services available at the institution that address a number of topics including mental health. There were several information posters on this bulletin board about activities happening on campus that week to support mental health. The fourth picture was a display case outside the intercultural centre that provided information on festivals and celebrations from all around the world. This display case had art (origami) hanging. The fifth picture was a poster advertising a mobile food market that takes place weekly on campus. The sixth picture was of downtown high-rise buildings and how they were all connected through pedways. The seventh picture was of several pieces of diverse art displayed in the institution. The eighth picture was a rainbow-coloured pole. Finally, the ninth picture was a computer lab in the institution.

Marlen. The fifth leader was Marlen, a manager in international education. I met with Marlen in her workplace office. What struck me the most was that within a few minutes of us introducing each other, Marlen shared her racial and ethnic background with me. She shared where her parents had emigrated from and the reasons they left their homeland. She also shared her family's religious background and where she was born. Marlen identified as a brown female. Opening in this way allowed for our conversation to explore how her sociohistorical background was intricately woven into her identity and role as a leader. Marlen was the first participant to openly declare and identify herself as a person of colour.

Marlen shared that she had been in various leadership roles and in various departments in the institution. In her current role, she interacts with a number of external stakeholders. Some of her tasks include providing training opportunities on matters of diversity and inclusivity to members of other postsecondary institutions. For Marlen, diversity and inclusivity mean

> we're in a space right now and I think Barack Obama spoke to it as being call-out culture where we've gone from this one space of "How do we ensure representation? How do we ensure voices are heard?" to a place where even I have found, I've kind of gone to where it's "If it's not right the first time, it's offensive." You know, I feel like this space of diversity and inclusion is always evolving.

Remarkably, Marlen did not provide an artifact. She, however, described her image of diversity and inclusivity in postsecondary as the organizational chart. She shared that "for me, I think that images of diversity at an institutional level are your org chart and what does that look like."

John Thomas. The sixth leader was John Thomas, an associate dean in the faculty of science. John Thomas identified as a black male. The interview with

John Thomas took place in a boardroom at the institution. Though this type of setting creates a sense of formality, John Thomas appeared to be relaxed and open to sharing his understanding of the concepts of diversity and inclusivity as they relate to the institution's strategic plan. I felt, however, that I did have to probe and push him a little to share his personal experiences with diversity and inclusivity as a leader in a postsecondary setting.

At the time of the interview, he had held a leadership position in the faculty for several years. As an associate dean, his role includes implementing the institutional strategic plan in the faculty and in the specific departments in his portfolio. He works directly with teaching faculty and nonfaculty members from other departments. For John Thomas, diversity and inclusivity in postsecondary education is a focus on the goal for "all learners to be able to learn what we present them, irrespective of their age, their gender, their race, their physical impairments or whether they're blind or whether they can hear properly and even cognitive impairment." The image John Thomas provided is of different adult learners sitting around a table using various electronic devices. According to John Thomas, this image depicted the following:

> What we are trying to do is, we are trying to allow our content to be accessible to learners of all forms, shapes, and sizes. We want them to be able to access our content and acquire from it exactly the maximum amount of information that we would like, using all means of delivery.

RNH. The seventh leader was RNH, a director of marketing and student recruitment. RNH identified as a brown male. The interview with RNH took place virtually on Zoom. This was the modality he preferred given time constraints. RNH participated in the video conference from his workplace office, and I participated from my home office. I was a little nervous about conducting the interview over Zoom as I was concerned about potential technical failures. Before the interview, I practiced recording a video meeting on Zoom and downloading the recorded video as an audio for transcription purposes. Fortunately, there were not any technical failures and the interview proceeded smoothly. RNH appeared to be very comfortable sharing his experiences on a virtual platform.

I was very excited to have a conversation with RNH because he worked in a marketing and recruitment department, which is very different from teaching and learning faculties. Like Marlen, RNH openly shared and declared he was a person of colour, and thus different in this respect from his colleagues in the institution's senior leadership positions. I was curious to hear his perspectives on diversity and inclusivity and explore how they related to those of the other participants. I found that some of his experiences as a senior leader resonated with mine. In such instances, I had to remind myself of my facial expressions during the interview and what messages they might convey. Not all of RNH's experiences or ideas, however, resonated with mine. Where there was dissonance, I had to make a mental effort to not show surprise. I found, during this Zoom interview, that I worked harder at monitoring my facial expressions than I did with the in-person interviews.

At the time of the interview, RNH had been in the role for a year and a half. Prior to joining the postsecondary institution, RNH worked in corporate settings. For RNH, diversity and inclusivity mean

> equal opportunity and the assessment of someone's merit based on skill only and experience and background and not necessarily other factors. So, I think equality speaks the most now and I do think it's important that a group or a team is well represented… in terms of diversity because I do think that cultural, spiritual, racial teachings and experience also factor in…. It helps build perspective.

RNH shared an image of a tree with many colourful leaves. For RNH, a tree is "like the universal sign of growth and strength." The role of postsecondary institutions is to cultivate the tree. He further shared,

> I love trees because they're grounded as well. So, it shows that you're able to grow in whatever which direction that you like to grow. You can grow whatever colour you'd like to grow in, but … never to lose sight of the fact that you should be grounded and that there's a foundation that you need to support.

Alex. The eighth leader was Alex, a program chair in the community studies department of her institution. Alex identified as a white female. My conversation with Alex took place on the Zoom virtual platform. She was in her workplace office, and I was in my home office. The virtual interview took place due to geographical location. This was my second virtual interview, and I felt more confident with the technology than I had in the first interview. Alex appeared to be very comfortable in the setting. She was willing to share her personal background experiences openly in order for me to have a frame of reference for her perspectives on diversity and inclusivity. I noticed that Alex was wearing a rainbow lanyard. She alluded to this lanyard in the conversation and explained that she wore it to signal to others she interacts with all and accepts diversity and inclusivity.

Alex shared that in her role as program chair, she interacts directly with teaching faculty and students in her Faculty and with those in other departments in the institution. For Alex, diversity is about "how people think and how they interact, how they perceive, how they develop relationships, how they form conclusions, or what they're curious about. I think those things all speak to me about what diversity is." Inclusivity to her is about "how are we accommodating or making room for these diverse opinions, thoughts, behaviours of others so that everybody can bring value and also respect to the things, the business of what we're doing."

Alex's artifact was an image of a bookshelf that has several shelves housing a variety of books that vary in size, colour, and type. Not all the books were neatly ordered and arranged. There were other objects on the bookshelf as well such as toys and pictures. For Alex, the bookshelf image communicates the reality that there is "every intention of this being a bookshelf, every intention of this being an institution, but you can't order it so that everything looks the same and everybody is the same. It can't be ordered that way."

Renee. The ninth leader was Renee, a vice-president overseeing the student life and learning portfolio at her institution. Renee identified as a white female. The interview was conducted using Zoom due to COVID-19 restrictions. At the time the interview took place, postsecondary institutions in Alberta had closed campuses. Students, faculty, and staff engaged in online interactions. Renee participated in the video conference from her home office. Likewise, I was in my home office. Similar to the previous video conference interviews I had conducted, I appreciated that the participants had their cameras turned on so we could see each other. Renee appeared calm and comfortable. She surprised me at the beginning of the interview by asking me a number of questions regarding my research interest and occupation. It was clear to me that she wanted to understand why I had decided to research the concepts of diversity and inclusivity. She expressed her appreciation for doctoral research given that she too had been through the experience of being a doctoral student. Like Alex and Marlen, Renee shared her personal background experiences in the form of stories so that I could get an appreciation of how she conceptualizes diversity and inclusivity in the postsecondary context.

In her role as vice-president, Renee interacts with several leaders from various faculties and departments in the institution. She also interacts with external stakeholders. She is involved in the creation of policies and procedures pertaining to student life in the institution. Diversity for Renee is about "representation of traits.... So, things like gender, sexual orientation, ability and disability, ethnicity, sort of just broadly that piece of capturing what the world actually looks like." She described inclusivity like this:

> It's not enough to just have the representation, but it has to be meaningful, engaged and that they're in an environment or an institution that is welcoming and that there is a sense of belonging and connection and community.

To demonstrate diversity and inclusivity in postsecondary education, Renee shared a picture of the institution's women's soccer team posing with the local city men's soccer club. Some soccer players in the photo were holding pink banners with the words "I am HeForShe" written on them. The photo was taken after a soccer match between the two teams. According to Renee, "the whole idea behind this movement is that it's men promoting gender equality. And there again was such good response from the campus community."

Conclusion

In this chapter I described my positionality as a researcher and a postsecondary leader. I sought to understand how postsecondary leaders who have made public commitments to values of diversity and inclusivity in Alberta make meaning of these concepts in their leadership practice in the current context. I also provided background information and context leading to the research study. I came to this research study with assumptions on leadership and educational outcomes, leadership and organizational culture, and finally leadership and student learning experiences. Finally, I introduced the leaders who participated in the study by sharing their profiles. In Chapter 2, I share what I learned on the topic of diversity and inclusivity from other educational and organizational culture researchers. In Chapter 3 and subsequent chapters, I describe and interpret the themes that arose from my conversations with the leaders. These themes reflect how postsecondary leaders understand, interpret, and enact values of diversity and inclusivity in educational settings. I then discuss the discursive limitations of diversity and inclusivity. I conclude with recommendations on how leaders can position themselves and the institutions they lead in ways that attend to equity and social justice concerns.

References

Ahmed, S. (2012). *On being included: Racism and diversity in institutional life.* Duke University Press.

Burke, L. (2013). Why we can't wait: Diversity planning in community colleges. *Community College Journal of Research and Practice, 37*(11), 839–843. https://doi.org/10.1080/106689 21003744934

Burnett, S.-A., & Huisman, J. (2010). Universities' responses to globalization: The influence of organizational culture. *Journal of Studies in International Education, 14*(2), 117–142. https://doi.org/10.1177/1028315309350717

Byron, J. (2002). What should students be entitled to expect from universities?: A postgraduate perspective. In OECD Programme on Institutional Management in Higher Education (Ed.), *Responding to student expectations* (pp. 45–52). Organisation for Economic Co-operation Development.

Crotty, M. (1998). *The foundations of social research: Meaning and perspective in the research process*. Sage Publications.

Dei, G. (2000). Towards an Anti-racism discursive framework. In G. S. Dei & A. Calliste (Eds.), *Power, knowledge and anti-racist education* (pp. 23–40). Fernwood Publishing.

Dei, G. J. (2014). Personal reflections on anti-racism education for a global context. *Encounters on Education, 15,* 239–249.

Dei, G. J. S., & Asgharzadeh, A. (2017). Inclusive education and social development in an African context. *Comparative and International Education Society of Canada, 33*(2), 2–16. https://doi.org/10.5206/cie-eci.v33i2.9041

DeLuca, C. (2013). Toward an interdisciplinary framework for educational inclusivity. *Canadian Journal of Education, 36*(1), 305–348.

Dimmock, C., & Walker, A. (2005). *Educational leadership culture and diversity*. Sage Publications.

Eastman, J. A. (2006). Revenue generation and organizational change in higher education: Insights from Canada. *Higher Education Management & Policy, 18*(3), 1–27.

Edmonston, B. (2016). Canada's immigration trends and patterns. *Canadian Studies in Population, 43*(1–2), 78–116. https://doi.org/10.25336/P64609

Elam, C., & Brown, G. (2005). The inclusive university: Helping minority students choose a college and identify institutions that value diversity. *Journal of College Admission, 187,* 14–17.

El-Assal, K. (2018). *How will immigration affect Canada's economic growth?* https://www.conferenceboard.ca/e-library/abstract.aspx?did=9667

Foreign Affairs, Trade and Development Canada. (2014). *Canada's International Education Strategy: Harnessing our knowledge advantage to drive innovation and prosperity*. https://international.gc.ca/global-markets-marches-mondiaux/assets/pdfs/overview-apercu-eng.pdf

Hughes, B. (2015). Recruiting, retaining, and benefiting from a diverse community college faculty: A case study of one college's successes. *Community College Journal of Research and Practice, 39*(7), 659–672. https://doi.org/10.1080/10668926.2014.885401

Immigration, Refugees and Citizenship Canada. (2018). *Annual report to Parliament on immigration*. https://www.canada.ca/content/dam/ircc/migration/ircc/english/pdf/pub/annual-report-2018.pdf

James, C. E. (2011a, May 15). Canada: Paradoxes of 'visible minorities' in job ads. *University World News.* https://www.universityworldnews.com/post.php?story=20110513185935314

James, C. E. (2011b, December 2). Isn't it about time we admit race matters? *EdCan Network.* https://www.edcan.ca/articles/isnt-it-about-time-we-admit-that-race-matters/

Jeffcoat, K., & Piland, W. E. (2012). Anatomy of a community college faculty diversity program. *Community College Journal of Research and Practice, 36*(6), 397–410. https://doi.org/10.1080/10668920902813477

Lopez, A. E. (2016). *Culturally responsive and socially just leadership: From theory to action.* Palgrave MacMillan

Lopez, A. E. (2020). Reflection: Harnessing energy of social movements for lasting change. *Multicultural Perspectives, 22*(3), 115–117. https://doi.org/10.1080/15210960.2020.1794467

Lopez. A. E. (2021). Examining alternative school leadership practices and approaches: A decolonising school leadership approach. *Intercultural Education.* https://doi.org/10.1080/14675986.2021.1889471

Lopez, A. E., & Olan, E. L. (2018). *Transformative pedagogies for teacher education: Moving towards critical praxis in an era of change.* Information Age Publishing.

Lopez, A. E., & Olan, E. L. (2019). *Transformative pedagogies for teacher education: Critical action, agency, and dialogue in teaching and learning contexts.* Information Age Publishing.

Northouse, P. (2016). *Leadership: Theory and practice.* Sage Publications.

Oliveras-Ortiz, Y., & Jones, J. S. (2016). An intellectual space for educational leaders' diversity and social justice discourse. *Diversity, Social Justice and the Educational Leader, 1*(1), 1–4.

Smith, M. (2017). Disciplinary silences: Race, indigeneity, and gender in the social sciences. In F. Henry, E. Dua, C. E. James, A. Kobayashi, P. Li, H. Ramos, & M. S. Smith (Eds.), *The equity myth: Racialization and indigeneity at Canadian Universities* (pp. 239–262). University of British Columbia Press.

Smith, M. (2019). *The diversity gap in 2019: Canadian U15 universities – Leadership pipeline.* Academic Women's Association, University of Alberta. https://uofaawa.files.wordpress.com/2019/06/2019_u15_leadership_diversity_gap_release_20jun2019_final-1.pdf

Walker, A., & Riordan, G. (2010). Leading collective capacity in culturally diverse schools. *School Leadership & Management, 30*(1), 51–63. https://doi.org/10.1080/13632430903509766

Wolfe, B. L., & Dilworth, P. (2015). Transitioning normalcy: Organizational culture, African American administrators, and diversity leadership in higher education. *Review of Educational Research, 85*(4), 667–697. https://doi.org/10.3102/0034654314565667

Zembylas, M., & Iasonos, S. (2010). Leadership styles and multicultural education approaches: An exploration of their relationship. *International Journal of Leadership in Education, 13*(2), 163–183. https://doi.org/10.1080/13603120903386969

· 2 ·

TOWARD THE INTEGRATED SOCIAL JUSTICE LEADERSHIP FRAMEWORK FOR DIVERSITY AND INCLUSIVITY

Introduction

There is a plethora of definitions and frameworks for diversity, inclusion, leadership and social justice. In this chapter I explore some of the definitions and frameworks that I think contribute to understanding how educational leaders navigate diversity and inclusivity. I share the varying definitions and conceptualizations of diversity, inclusivity, organizational culture, and leadership. I also share the various diversity and inclusion frameworks that have been developed by researchers. In exploring these various frameworks and in dialogue with the postsecondary leaders who participated in my research study, I came to realize that there was a need to engage a wholistic framework that was reflective of the realities of educational leaders, practitioners, in the current context. To this end, I developed the integrated social justice leadership framework for diversity and inclusivity to gain insight into how leaders understand themselves, their leadership practice, and their ecosystem in relation to diversity and inclusivity. I introduce the integrated social justice leadership framework for diversity and inclusivity toward the end of this chapter.

Diversity

Diversity is complex and does not carry a single conceptualization. Conceptualizations of diversity range from physical characteristics to attitudes and ideas. A broader definition of diversity that goes beyond visible characteristics such as race and gender is befitting given the intersectionality in people's identities. As Castania (1996) pointed out, all individuals have the experience of being in both dominant and excluded groups. This is supported by scholars (Castania, 1996) who have argued for studying diversity through a lens of power. In this section, I explore how diversity has been defined and conceptualized by various scholars. I draw from scholars in the field of education as well as organizational studies. The reason I draw from these two fields is that my research was situated in organizations that provide education. After providing the definitions and conceptualization of diversity, I describe the debates in the literature on diversity. From there, I report on what the literature describes as the benefits of diversity.

Defining Diversity. The meaning and conceptualization of diversity varies across institutions and individuals. Lopez and Olan (2018) defined diversity simply as the various ways that people identify themselves. The Cornell Cooperative Extension defined diversity as "differences among people with respect to age, class, ethnicity, gender, physical and mental ability, race, sexual orientation, spiritual practice, and other human differences" (Castania, 1996, p. 1). Aguirre and Martinez (2002) defined diversity as "multiple types of communities based on cultural, racial, ethnic or sexual identities" (p. 54). Corporate companies, such as Deloitte, extended the definition of diversity to include "diversity of thought, perspectives, and life experiences which may include education, family status, values and beliefs, working-style preferences, and socioeconomic status" (Sherman Garr et al., 2014, p. 11). Ahmed (2012), a critical race and social justice scholar, stated that diversity "involves the aesthetic realm of appearance, as well as the moral realm of value. It creates a body that can be seen and valued as a diverse body" (p. 59).

In a review of organization studies literature on diversity, Janssens and Steyaert (2003) observed that diversity has been conceptualized from a moral or ethical perspective and from an organizational or economical perspective. Moral-ethical perspective studies attend to issues of inequality in organizations and are emancipatory in nature. These studies "seek a more socially just situation in which the available functions and positions are spread more evenly over the different groups" (Janssens & Steyaert, 2003, p. 2). From an organizational or economical perspective, diversity has been categorized according to three dimensions: cultural, functional, and historical. The cultural dimension of diversity refers to religion, age, ethnicity, and language, whereas the functional dimension of diversity refers to differences in the way people think, learn, process information, and deal with authority. The historical dimension of diversity considers family make-up, political opinions, and intergroup relationships. Another categorization of diversity common in organization studies initiated by McGrath et al. (1995, as cited in Janssens & Steyaert, 2003) has five groupings: demographic characteristics; task-related knowledge, skills, and capacities; values, views, and attitudes; personality, and cognitive and attitudinal styles; and status in the organization.

Social justice and critical race scholars have asserted that the use of the word "diversity" in institutions has replaced discussion of race and racism (Ahmed, 2012; Dei, 2000, 2014; James, 2011b). These scholars maintained that the word "diversity" is considered a safe word or a good public relations word, which, unfortunately, masks issues of race and racism. Dei (2000) stated that the dominant discourse in Canadian society is white and Christian. Matters of diversity should require that one addresses "questions of equity and power-sharing within a social context that sees Whiteness as the norm" (Dei, 2000, p. 27). To attend to questions of diversity, Dei (2000) presented an anti-racist discursive framework, which serves to do the following:

- examine structural barriers to and social practices for systemic change,
- question the marginalization of certain voices in society,
- challenge what constitutes valid knowledge and how knowledge is produced,
- engage in issues of representation and the need to have multiple voices and perspectives in mainstream knowledge production,
- acknowledge the need for a more inclusive social system that can respond to the needs of minorities, and
- question institutional response to diversity and difference. (p. 34)

Diversity and difference are defined as "the intersections of race, gender, class, sexuality, language, culture and religion" (Dei, 2000, p. 34). Individuals have multiple and intersecting identities, and "these identities are also sites of shifting power relations that inform, constrain and determine the human experience and condition" (Dei, 2000, p. 31). According to Dei (2014), race is "a subjective identity marker and lived experience that exceeds the limits of scientific, natural, fixed, and bounded categories ... [and it] speaks of socio-historical processes and human social condition" (p. 240).

Diversity Debates. With such varying definitions of diversity, it is not surprising that there is not agreement among scholars on the conceptualization of diversity. Four themes have emerged from debates on diversity as follows: "a narrow or broad definition of diversity, a stable or dynamic conception of identity, the role of power, and the importance of the socio-historical context" (Janssens & Steyaert, 2003, p. 12). In the debate on defining diversity, scholars who were in favour of a narrow definition of diversity argued that it should be limited to specific cultural categories. These scholars maintained that "diversity based on race, ethnicity and gender cannot be understood in the same way as diversity based upon organizational functions, abilities or cognitive orientations" (Nkomo, 1995, as cited in Janssens & Steyaert, 2003, p. 12). On the other side of the debate were scholars in favour of a broader definition of diversity that goes beyond demographic characteristics. These scholars argued that an "individual has multiple identities and that the multiple dimensions cannot be isolated in an organizational setting" (Janssens & Steyaert, 2003, p. 13).

In the debate on the conception of identity within diversity literature, some scholars argued that people "identify directly to the social category they belong to on the basis of their individual characteristics" (Janssens & Steyaert, 2003, p. 14). From this perspective, a person's identity is stable, fixed, and consistent. Contrary to this perspective is the view that identity is "best seen as a set of contradictory, fluid, contextual constrained positions within which people are capable of exercising choice" (Ely, 1995, as cited in Janssens & Steyaert, 2003, p. 14). A person's identity is dynamic and fluid.

The third theme that emerged in the debates on diversity identified by Janssens and Steyaert (2003) is that of the role of power. Power inequalities and sociohistorical context must be considered when studying diversity. When power is placed at the centre of an approach to diversity, then diversity ceases to be perceived as a set of attributes; rather, diversity is understood as a condition of a relationship (Ely, 1995, as cited in Janssens & Steyaert, 2003, p. 16).

The final theme to emerge from the debates on diversity is the significance of the sociohistorical context of diversity. To understand diversity in the workplace, it is crucial to factor in the sociohistorical context given that "occupational roles tend to be segregated by race or by gender on the basis of assumptions about race- or gender-related competencies, having their roots in the history of the labor market and in differences in educational opportunities" (Janssens & Steyaert, 2003, p. 16).

Not having a shared understanding of what diversity means results in problematic definitions such as "counting people who look different" (Ahmed, 2012, p. 79). Ahmed's (2012) research showed that the word "diversity" is a comfortable word for people to use. Unlike words such as "inequity," "inequality," and "social justice," "diversity" is viewed as nonthreatening. James (2011b) alluded to diversity as "a code word for race" (p. 2). This presents a challenge. According to Ahmed,

> the fact that diversity is not a scary word is part of the problem: if it is detached from scary issues, such as power and inequality, it is harder for diversity to do anything in its travels. What happens when the words we use allow us to pass over the reasons we use them? What happens when words become comfortable? (2012, p. 66)

Diversity practitioners in Ahmed's research shared their awareness of the positivity around the word "diversity," and for some it is a positive word that they use as a tool to accomplish their work. For others, the word "diversity can allow organizations to retain their good idea of themselves ... it gives permission to those working within institutions to turn away from ongoing realities of institutional inequality" (Ahmed, 2012, p. 71). Ahmed shared an example of how the positive language of diversity is used in institutional responses to allegations of racism and can be a way to maintain public relations: "Diversity as public relations can thus be mobilized in defense of an organization and its reputation" (2012, p. 144). Unfortunately, this glosses over the inequality issues in the institution.

Benefits of Diversity in Education. In Chapter 1, I shared my assumptions for this study. One of my assumptions was that diversity in leadership benefits higher education in that learning becomes more accessible and teaching methods become more inclusive of diverse learner needs (Lopez, 2016; Walker & Riordan, 2010; Wolfe & Dilworth, 2015). In a study to examine the relationship between faculty diversity and graduation rates in higher education in the United States, Stout et al. (2018) found that the greater the diversity among faculty, the higher the graduation rates for all underrepresented minority (URM) students. The researchers suggested that "as organizational-level compositional diversity increases, students, especially URM students, feel a better fit with their environments and therefore achieve at a higher level, leading to increased graduation rates" (Stout et al., 2018, p. 403). Elam and Brown (2005) declared that cultural diversity on campus is important given that it allows for multicultural education and a challenging of stereotypes. The authors supported the notion that "curricula that bring students from diverse backgrounds together to grapple with current social issues can promote constructive interactions that increase understanding, decrease prejudicial attitudes, and foster development of attitudes regarding social justice" (Smith, 1997, as cited in Elam & Brown, 2005, p. 15). Such an awareness and building of knowledge benefits society (Burke, 2013).

Inclusivity in Education

The demographic makeup of students in postsecondary institutions is shifting. This driver for change requires institutions to reexamine how they make meaning of diversity in order to ensure that all learners are included. An educational experience that is inclusive is one in which the diversity of the learners is embraced and reflected in the curriculum content and delivery as well as the learning environment.

In this section, I explore the meaning, importance, and challenges of inclusivity in the field of education. I highlight the challenges brought forward in the literature of defining inclusivity in education as well as the challenges that unconscious frames of reference, also referred to as implicit bias, present with regard to inclusivity. I then present a framework that scholars have provided for analyzing inclusivity in education. I conclude the section with a discussion on the connection between diversity and inclusivity in postsecondary education.

Defining Inclusivity in Education. Usually, inclusivity in education is associated with educational programming for students with "special needs." However, Alberta Education (n.d.) defined inclusion as

> a way of thinking and acting that demonstrates universal acceptance and promotes a sense of belonging for all learners.... Inclusion is not just about learners with special needs. It is an attitude and approach that embraces diversity and learner differences and promotes equal opportunities for all learners in Alberta. (paras. 1–2)

In this research, inclusivity in education encompasses the various dimensions of diversity. I take up the definition provided by Alberta Education (as cited in Williamson & Gilham, 2014) that "inclusion in the education system is about ensuring that each student belongs and receives a quality education no matter their ability, disability, language, cultural background, gender, or age" (p. 558). I find that this definition is also applicable to the postsecondary context.

The UNESCO (1994, as cited in Loreman, 2014) Salamanca Statement noted that "inclusive education systems provide ... the most effective means of combating discriminatory attitudes, creating welcoming communities, building an inclusive society and achieving education for all" (p. 459). To achieve an inclusive education system, Alberta Education (n.d.) listed six principles to guide and inform policy, practices, and actions: anticipate, value, and support diversity and learner differences; high expectations for all learners; understand learners' strengths and needs; remove barriers within learning environments; build capacity; and collaborate for success. According to the Alberta School Councils' Association (2019), educators need to "identify and reduce barriers within the curriculum, the learning environment and/or instruction that are interfering with students' ability to be successful learners and to participate in the school community" (Principles of Inclusive Education section, para. 4). Furthermore, capacity building refers to the opportunities and resources that all education professionals (e.g., leaders, teachers) need to have in order to "develop, strengthen and renew their understanding, skills and abilities to create flexible and responsive learning environments. Capacity building takes place at the personal, school and system levels" (Alberta School Councils' Association, 2019, Principles of Inclusive Education section, para. 5).

Shields (2002) explored the following four values needed for the development of inclusive school communities: developing respect, eliminating power inequities, embracing diverse perspectives, and establishing high expectations for all students. These four values are encapsulated in Alberta Education's (n.d.) six principles of inclusive education. Removing barriers that interfere with students' ability to be successful and to participate in the campus community aligns with the value of eliminating power inequities. Eliminating power inequities calls for the acknowledgement that these inequities exist in curriculum (Shields, 2002; Smith et al., 2017). The curricula of a number of Western countries tend "to be linear, inflexible, divorced from context, overly specific, centralized, and unresponsive to the needs of minority groups" (Goodman & Bond, 1993, as cited in Loreman, 2007, p. 28). Similarly, other scholars stated that the present-day curriculum "is designed primarily to reproduce the inequality of social classes while it mostly benefits the interests of the dominant class" (Macedo, 1995, as cited in Shields, 2002, p. 227). Meeting the needs of the various subcultures present in educational institutions today requires Shield's third value of embracing diverse perspectives through multi-cultural education.

Historically "multicultural education initially referred to demands for school reform articulated first by African Americans, then by other groups of color, followed by women, people with disabilities, and gay rights advocates" (McLaren, 1995, as cited in Shields, 2002, p. 228). Multicultural education now encapsulates various dimensions of diversity found in educational institutions. Multicultural education is "an approach to teaching and student learning that encourages cultural pluralism within culturally diverse societies in a world that is becoming more global" (Burke, 2013, p. 842). For an institution to be inclusive, its leaders need to foster multicultural education and inclusive environments where students are exposed to various dimensions of diversity (Burke, 2013).

Engaging students in multicultural education needs to go beyond celebrating cultural artifacts if inclusivity in education is to be achieved. In Canada, the Multiculturalism Act of 1988 serves to encourage the various cultural groups in Canada to observe their cultural practices, honour their ancestry, maintain their cultural identities, and still be considered equal members of Canadian society (Lopez, 2017a). A challenge presented by the Multiculturalism Act is that it "is reflective of the deeply held belief among most Canadians that the society is 'culturally neutral'" (James, 2011c, p. 194). The perception of neutrality is problematic, particularly in education, as it means that structural inequalities are not addressed. The curriculum and pedagogy in the Canadian education system reflects the dominant white and Eurocentric perspective. James (2011c) stated that "education in Canada is mired in a color-blind and monocultural discourse in terms of vision, content and style that the promise of democracy, inclusivity and equity continue to elude minority students" (p. 192).

St. Denis (2011), a critical race and First Nation scholar, agreed with James' (2011c) position on multiculturalism and stated that "public schools are defended as neutral multicultural spaces where all participants are equally positioned, irrespective of racism and colonialism" (p. 313). She similarly argued that multiculturalism does not address issues of racism and structural inequality in the education system and in society at large particularly for Indigenous groups. Instead, "multiculturalism is a form of colonialism and works to distract from the recognition and redress of Indigenous rights" (St. Denis, 2011, p. 308). St. Denis further argued that discourses of multiculturalism give the illusion of fairness, tolerance, and innocence. Furthermore, in a multiculturalism framework, Indigenous perspectives are but one perspective among many: "Multiculturalism in schools makes it possible for non-Aboriginal teachers and schools to trivialize Aboriginal content and perspectives, and at the same time believe that they are becoming more inclusive and respectful" (St. Denis, 2011, p. 313).

Interdisciplinary Framework for Educational Inclusion. There is ambiguity in the meaning of inclusion in Canada and a contributing factor to this ambiguity in the field of education is "that inclusive research and policy initiatives have stemmed from a range of sub-disciplines: special education and disability studies, multiculturalism and anti-racist education, gender and women's studies, and queer studies" (DeLuca, 2013, p. 308). In response to the need for a Canadian framework that can be used in reference to inclusivity matters across various disciplines, DeLuca (2013) developed an interdisciplinary framework for educational inclusion, which "is intended to represent multiple forms of inclusivity to edify historical, existing, and idealistic educational practices and structures, allowing for the identification and positioning of various responses to diversity" (p. 308).

This interdisciplinary framework for educational inclusivity characterizes four approaches to diversity and inclusivity that lie on a continuum: normative, integrative, dialogical, and transgressive. Normative inclusivity is the "active assimilation and normalization of minority individuals to a dominant cultural standard" (DeLuca, 2013, p. 326). Integrative inclusivity "accepts and legitimizes the presence of difference within society and learning environments through formal institutional modifications" (DeLuca, 2013, p. 330). In this conception, difference is recognized and a dominant culture exists. Dialogical inclusivity recognizes that people are culturally complex. In this conception, a dominant group still exists; "however, the dominant group honours, welcomes, and celebrates the cultural complexity of individuals" (DeLuca, 2013, p. 332). Transgressive inclusivity uses diversity "as a vehicle for the generation of new knowledge and learning experiences" (DeLuca, 2013, p. 334).

Power is conceptualized in the framework "along a continuum from unicentric to multicentric to concentric" (DeLuca, 2013, p. 325). In the unicentric conceptualization, the dominant group holds power; this is a normative approach to inclusivity. In a multicentric conceptualization, a dominant group exists but power relationships are asymmetrical and circulating. A multicentric approach reflects an integrative and dialogical approach to inclusivity where difference is acknowledged. Finally, in a concentric conceptualization, "all individuals are recognized as culturally complex with a shared power relationship" (DeLuca, 2013, p. 325).

In thinking through the interdisciplinary framework for educational inclusivity, DeLuca (2013) referenced the integrative framework of inclusive education (Dei et al., 2000). Though the integrative framework for inclusive education stems from multicultural education and antiracist education disciplines, it "represents a critical shift that moves the discourse of inclusivity away from advocacy for individual groups toward a discourse of plurality and multiplicity," according to DeLuca (2013, p. 315). Dei et al. (2000) argued for an approach to inclusivity that "accepts indigenous and cultural knowledge alongside the dominant culture with the aim of creating spaces for the sharing and exchange of different ways of knowing" (p. 316). This approach calls for a focus on power relations in education and for educational leaders to attend to issues of power.

However, DeLuca (2013) argued that Dei et al.'s (2000) approach to inclusivity "simplifies hegemony within the cultural complexity of contemporary social interactions" (p. 323). Dei et al. viewed power as hierarchical and dualistic, where the oppressor is in opposition to the oppressed. DeLuca pointed out that there is a continuum on which power relations exist. On one end of the continuum is a unicentric hegemonic relationship in which one group has power over another. In this unicentric power relationship, the dominant group is at the centre of the relationship, and nondominant groups are expected to assimilate to the dominant culture. Following this is a multicentric hegemonic relationship where a dominant group still holds power but is not at the centre of the relationship. There is a recognition of diverse groups and institutions modify the learning environment to accommodate the needs of different groups. An example of modifications is streaming students whose first language is not English. At the end of the continuum is a concentric hegemonic relationship where power is shared equally among the various groups. For DeLuca, the concentric hegemonic relationship, where power relationships are not dualistic, is ideal for inclusivity. Diversity in the learner population is used to generate new knowledge and experiences.

The interdisciplinary framework for educational inclusivity "applies to all groups of difference and serves to bridge identities related to, but not limited to gender, social class, race/ethnicity, religion, ability, nationality, sexual orientation, and interest" (DeLuca, 2013, p. 324). The interdisciplinary framework for educational inclusivity and the integrative framework for inclusive education are similar in that both were designed to appeal to different groups.

However, DeLuca (2013) indicated that the interdisciplinary framework for educational inclusivity is not linked "to an existing theoretical framework associated with any historically marginalized group. In this way, the theory is intended to hold appeal and value for all groups and for theorizing inclusivity as a transdisciplinary practice" (pp. 324–325). I would argue that it is important to engage with diversity and inclusivity from a critical perspective if oppressive practices that have historically excluded marginalized students are to be challenged.

Implicit Bias

An educator's unconscious or implicit bias, in itself a risk to inclusivity efforts in education, has been defined as a "hidden or unintentional preference for a particular group based on social identity such as race, gender, class, ability, or sexual orientation … originating in the unconscious mind" (Choudhury, 2015, as cited in Smith et al., 2017, p. 264). Drago-Severson and Blum-DeStefano (2017) acknowledged that educators have "orientations toward race, diversity, identity, privilege, and collaboration across lines of difference," where orientations are defined as "the powerful and often unconscious dispositions that guide our thinking, feeling, and acting in relation to our own and others' identity, our work, and societal demands more broadly" (p. 460). Despite educators professing to have values of diversity and inclusivity, implicit bias can impede teaching and leadership outcomes in educational settings (Drago-Severson & Blum DeStefano, 2017).

Smith et al. (2017) described 12 unconscious race and gender biases that negatively impact BIPOC educators in Canadian universities. When the implicit biases of decision-makers and those in positions of power are not acknowledged and addressed, the outcomes are unfairness and inequity for racialized and Indigenous individuals in several ways. Some of the implicit biases that Smith et al. (2017) described and that are of interest to this study are canonical and curriculum biases, affinity bias and homosocial reproduction, resume racism, and accent bias.

As described earlier in this chapter, the curricula in countries such as Canada reflect the values, assumptions, and worldview of the dominant white Eurocentric culture (James, 2011c; Shohat & Stam, 2014). Smith et al. (2017) expressed the view that much of the modern disciplinary curriculum is white, Eurocentric, and colonial, and continues to reflect historical biases against women, indigenous and racialized scholars, and scholarship from non-Western countries, meaning that diverse histories and intellectual heritage continue to be invisible in disciplinary curricula. (p. 279)

Students from racialized, Indigenous, and minority backgrounds do not see themselves reflected in the curriculum (James, 2011c; Lopez & Olan, 2018; Loreman 2007; Shields, 2002; Smith et al., 2017) which is Eurocentric. The underpinning beliefs and values of the curriculum reflect white European ways of knowing which are so entrenched in daily routines that they are unnoticed and are the norm (Shohat & Stam, 2014). The absence of diverse perspectives in the curriculum and diverse ways of generating knowledge renders invisible the histories, experiences, and knowledge of underrepresented populations. This results in a continued power imbalance, unfairness, and inequity in the field of education. Furthermore, "racialized and indigenous students do not see themselves reflected in the University professoriate and leadership, and their histories and experiences are inadequately reflected in the curriculum, or in knowledge production and dissemination" (Smith et al., 2007, p. 262). It is important for educators to engage in disruptive pedagogy (Lopez & Olan, 2018) whereby they challenge the status quo and assumptions made in the curriculum they teach.

Research has shown that despite employment equity initiatives and statements, senior leadership in postsecondary institutions is predominantly white and male (James & Chapman-Nyaho, 2017; Smith, 2019). Affinity bias is a contributing factor to the disproportionate underrepresentation of minority populations in academic leadership positions (James & Chapman-Nyaho, 2017; Smith, 2017). Affinity bias and homosocial reproduction refer to the "preference for sameness … and practices that standardize, homogenize, and replicate specific bodies and bodies of knowledge" (Smith et al., 2017, p. 264). In a study on the experiences and perceptions of BIPOC faculty members on the impact their presence has had in their institutions, participants perceived that "hiring is often based on affinity groupings and appointment committee members' friendships networks. In other words, departments are 'cloning' themselves" (James & Chapman-Nyaho, 2017, p. 99). Participants shared their experiences in the hiring process at their institutions where decisions made were in favour of educational credentials from Canada and against non-Canadian immigration status and non-Anglo accents. Participants found the claims regarding "culture fit" and who was the "best candidate" as reasons for not hiring faculty from underrepresented populations troubling.

The various dimensions of diversity such as race, gender, class, sexual orientation, and more influence the hiring process (James, 2017). To claim neutrality and to deny one's implicit biases during recruitment and hiring is a positivist claim to objectivity. Participants in James and Chapman-Nyaho's (2017) study also shared that although their institutions had made public statements of commitment to equity and social justice, their colleagues were not willing to "accommodate their 'different' curriculum, scholarship, teaching approaches, and community service inclinations – in short, the diverse orientations of their work" (p. 104). These faculty were under pressure to conform to and uphold the status quo. Maintaining the status quo is what allows for the reproduction of inequity and exclusion despite commitments to values of diversity and inclusivity.

Organizational Culture

Two of the researcher assumptions I identified in Chapter 1 were that leaders help shape meaning and the culture of their organizations (Northouse, 2016; Zembylas & Iasonos, 2010) and that the culture in which leaders operate influences their leadership practices (Burke, 2013; Dimmock & Walker, 2005). I learned from the literature that it is possible to have a shift in organizational culture. For this cultural shift to happen, institutional leaders need to reconsider the organizational culture which informs their leadership practices (Wolfe & Dilworth, 2015) To this end, it was important for me to consider the culture of the institutions where participants in the current study practised leadership.

I begin this section by defining organizational culture and its significance. I then explore the relationship between diversity and the culture of educational institutions where diversity programs have been implemented. I also explore the perspectives of diversity practitioners in educational settings through the work of critical and social justice scholars Ahmed (2012) and Lopez (2016).

Defining Organizational Culture. Organizational culture and context are increasingly studied as concepts in school leadership and administration (Walker & Dimmock, 2002). Culture, along with other factors such as economic, sociological, political, demographic, and legislative, impact educational institutions. Walker and Dimmock (2002) stressed that the

> inclusion of the regional and local sub-cultural levels acknowledges that varying cultural configurations reside within broader societal cultures and that these can exert

significant influence on school organization, leadership, curriculum and learning and teaching. (p. 173)

It is necessary to develop an understanding of the cultural conditions within which leadership is practiced (Zembylas & Iasonos, 2010). Each institution has its own culture. Within that institutional culture exist subcultures that are defined by dimensions of diversity such as ethnicity, gender, religious affiliation, socioeconomic status, and many more. In order to be inclusive of the various subcultures that are present, "there is a need for institutions to reexamine the culture in which their leadership and traditions have been structured" (Wolfe & Dilworth, 2015, p. 685).

Organizational culture has been defined as "a combination of values, beliefs, language, rituals, and ideologies that are explicit and implicit through day-to-day practices within an organization" (Wolfe & Dilworth, 2015, p. 671). The culture and values of the dominant group are what is reflected on college campuses. This means that the day-to-day practices within an educational institution, be they implicit or explicit, reflect the dominant culture. Wolfe and Dilworth (2015) used critical race theory to bring to light practices that are defined as "normal" but are oppressive to marginalized groups. Critical race theory is a "race-centered theory, it helps validate the knowledge base and experiences that African Americans (and historically marginalized minorities) bring to research, and retheorize the Eurocentric male dominant discourse, which is often used to describe the experiences of people of colour" (Solorzano & Yosso, 2002, as cited in Wolfe & Dilworth, 2015, p. 678). It validates the experiences of marginalized populations and exposes "dominant norms and assumptions that appear neutral but systematically marginalize, silence, and misrepresent people of color" (Wolfe & Dilworth, 2015, p. 678). In their analysis, Wolfe and Dilworth identified, among other themes, the need for research on higher education administration in relation to underrepresented minority populations. They also stressed the need for research on diverse leadership with a focus on the experiences of underrepresented groups. They suggested that the idea of a diverse leadership challenges homogeneity and may not be compatible with the dominant organizational culture.

Organizational Culture and Diversity Planning. In response to the changing demographics on postsecondary campuses, Burke (2013) explored diversity planning as a key component of institutional effectiveness. According to Burke, "culturally competent institutions cultivate climates that support diversity leadership, institutional diversity planning, and multicultural education"

(2013, p. 840). In order for an institution to be culturally competent, its diversity initiatives need to transcend symbolic dimensions of diversity.

In a case study to explore how a community college diversified its faculty in ways that supported the institution's strategic goals and strengthened the institution, Hughes (2015) recommended three principles that colleges can use to achieve increased faculty diversity— namely, intentional action, strategic planning, and relationships. The formation of a Diversity Committee triggered a cultural shift at the community college in the case study. The committee was responsible for advocating that the college adapt and evolve in order to meet the needs of a changing student demographic. It also developed the college's Diversity Policy. Because of this policy, hiring criteria were established to assess a candidate's "experiences in fostering and maintaining a climate that valued diversity" (Hughes, 2015, p. 663). As a result of the policy, criteria that measured competency and experience in diversity planning were used to hire a new vice president. The newly appointed vice president then led a number of initiatives at the college that promoted sustainable faculty diversity.

Jeffcoat and Piland (2012) provided a description, analysis, and report on a faculty diversity internship program that was implemented in California. The goal of the program was to diversify the faculty in community colleges in the state. The dimensions of diversity addressed in this program were ethnicity and gender. Initiatives such as formal mentoring programs were implemented as part of the retention efforts in California. The formal mentoring helped bridge cross-cultural relationships. Jeffcoat and Piland considered the program a success and stated that more still needs to be done to increase ethnic diversity in college faculty.

Multiple and intersecting identities have an influence on attitudes and behaviours in organizations (Walker & Riordan, 2010) Leaders of culturally diverse schools need to negotiate intersectionality in order to build collective capacity in schools where there is a diverse staff. According to Walker and Riordan (2010), collective capacity is defined as "the ways people work together in schools to improve student learning and lives" (p. 51). This collective capacity relies on shared values and relationships. The ways people work together is greatly impacted by the culture of the organization in which they work. Educational leaders are a part of the culture of the organization. It is important that they too examine their beliefs and values when leading culturally diverse institutions. Diversity and inclusion in education require social justice leadership, which "enables questions to be asked about how social, political and economic advantages and disadvantages are replicated in school organizational structures and cultures" Zembylas & Iasonos, 2010, p. 165). Diversity and inclusion require critical leadership, whereby leaders "identify inequities and injustices that lead to the marginalization and exclusion of those who should be full participants in their organizations" (Shields, 2002, p. 219).

The diversity efforts reported by Burke (2013), Hughes (2015), and Jeffcoat and Piland (2012) require what Ahmed (2012) described as a willingness to challenge institutional whiteness. The dominant discourse in educational institutions in Canada is white, male, and Eurocentric (James, 2017; Lopez, 2016; Shohat & Stam, 2014; Smith, 2019). The need for initiatives to diversify faculty confirms that what is already in place and dominant is whiteness. In such cases, diversity means "the inclusion of people who look different" (Puwar, 2004, as cited in Ahmed, 2012, p. 33). Studies by scholars such as James (2017) and Lopez (2016) point to the challenges that BIPOC faculty face with regard to inclusivity in curriculum, ways of teaching, scholarship, and community service that is different from the "norm" and that reflects their identities and the needs of the diverse student body. Ahmed argued that those who embody diversity (look different) face a metaphorical "brick wall," referring to "that which keeps its place even when official commitment to diversity has been given" (2012, p. 174). Furthermore, "people of color are welcomed on *condition* they return that hospitality by integrating into a common organizational culture, or by being diverse, and allowing institutions to celebrate their diversity." (Ahmed, 2012, p. 43). Burke argued that diversity efforts need to surpass symbolic gestures to have cultural change in an organization.

Leadership in the Postsecondary Context

In Chapter 1, I listed a researcher assumption that leadership impacts educational outcomes (Lopez, 2020; Walker & Riordan, 2010). In this section, I explore leadership theories that are connected with change given the increasing diversity in the postsecondary student population. Though there are other leadership theories, I have chosen to review transformational leadership, adaptive leadership, and social justice leadership theories as they concern change. Demographic shifts and social justice pressures are drivers for change that impact higher education institutions and have implications for leadership practice.

Defining Leadership. Leadership has been defined and conceptualized in a number of ways in the 20th and 21st centuries. Scholars have not come up with a single definition or conceptualization of leadership given that it is complex and carries different meaning for different people; however, the main components of leadership found in most definitions are process, influence, groups, and common goals (Northouse, 2016). Ryan (2002) defined leadership as "the ways in which processes of influence work between and among individuals and groups" (p. 983). Leadership engages "a social influence process whereby intentional influence is exerted by one person (or group) over other people (or groups) to structure the activities and relationships in a group or organization" (Yukl, 1994, as quoted in Ryan, 2002, p. 983). Social justice and critical scholars Dei (2019), James (2019), and Lopez (2016, 2020, 2021) called for a critical reflection on the current conceptualizations of and approaches to leadership, which they stated are of a dominant Western worldview.

Student populations in educational institutions in North America in general are increasingly becoming diverse (Lopez, 2016; Shields, 2002; Wolfe & Dilworth, 2015). The demographic shift in educational institutions has resulted in shifts "with respect to dominant language, religion, values, beliefs, and practices" (Shields, 2002, p. 210). Demographic changes within the population are an indicator that "there is an ongoing need to plan for diverse leadership successions to guide institutions through transformational periods of increasingly multifaceted populations that will shift campus culture for years to come (Harvey, 2011, as cited in Wolfe & Dilworth, 2015, p. 686). Educational leaders are called "to find new, more accepting, more respectful and inclusive ways to respond to diversity ... to find new ways of thinking about and leading these complex school communities" (Shields, 2002, p. 213).

To explore the type of leadership needed to lead diverse higher education institutions in a way that is inclusive, I drew on transformational leadership theory and adaptive leadership theory, and social justice leadership theories. I recognize that there are other leadership theories that have been generated; however, for the purposes of my case study, where the phenomenon is diversity and inclusivity in a context of change, I advance these three leadership theories as they are theories that concern change.

Transformational Leadership. "Leadership in higher education is often viewed as transformational, meaning that it is responsive and adaptive to promoting change in the institution and its relationship with the surrounding environment" (Wolfe & Dilworth, 2015, p. 671). Transformational leadership is a popular leadership approach in a variety of fields including education. Its popularity is due to "its emphasis on intrinsic motivation and follower development, which fits the needs of today's work groups, who want to be inspired and empowered to success in times of uncertainty" (Bass & Riggio, 2006, as cited in Northouse, 2016, p. 161). Transformational leadership requires that a leader influences and moves followers to exceed expectations. This means that a transformational leader needs to be charismatic and visionary in order to motivate followers and inspire them to be more moral. There are four factors of transformational leadership: idealized influence, where leaders are seen as strong role models; inspirational motivation, where leaders inspire followers to exceed organizational expectations; intellectual stimulation, where leaders encourage creativity and innovation; and individualized consideration, where leaders pay attention to the needs of individual team members. Kouzes and Posner (2012) developed a model of transformational leadership that comprises five practices leaders need to perform: model the way, inspire a shared vision, challenge the process, enable others to act, and encourage the heart. "The transformational approach also requires that leaders become social architects. This means that they make clear the emerging values and norms of the organization. They involve themselves in the culture of the organization and help shape its meaning" (Northouse, 2016, p. 176).

The transformational leadership approach has several strengths (Northouse, 2016). First, the transformational approach has been researched from a variety of perspectives; as a result, there are data to support this approach. Second, transformational leadership is an appealing approach as it aligns with North American societal expectations of leadership, which, I note, are the dominant culture expectations of leadership. Third, it is an approach in which there is a developmental relationship between the leader and followers. Fourthly, transformational leadership focuses on developing the capacity of followers. A focus on the needs, values, and morals of the followers is yet another strength of this leadership approach. Lastly, research provides evidence that transformational leadership is an approach that is effective in organizations (Northouse, 2016, pp. 176–177).

Transformational leadership as an approach has weaknesses. Northouse (2016) referenced scholars who believe that it lacks conceptual clarity in that the similarities and differences between transformational leadership and managerial practices are not evident. Additionally, the validity of transformational leadership measurement scales has been questioned, as there has been no clear correlation between the four factors of transformational leadership. Another criticism of transformational leadership is that this approach is dependent on a leader's traits and personality (charisma). The challenge with this is that it implies that teaching people to become transformational leaders is not possible. A fourth criticism is that there is no evidence that transformational leadership actually causes changes in followers and in organizations. Some scholars such as Yukl (1999, as cited in Northouse, 2016) have accused transformational leadership of a "heroic bias" whereby attention on the reciprocal nature or shared leadership in the relationship between a leader and followers is not spotlighted. Lastly, there is the potential for abuse of power given that it is not clear who sets the vision and decides on the values that followers are to adopt. Northouse (2016) summarized that

> transformational leadership does not provide a clearly defined set of assumptions about how leaders should act in a particular situation to be successful. Rather, it provides a general way of thinking about leadership that emphasized ideals, inspiration, innovations, and individual concerns. (p. 180)

The literature on transformational leadership indicated that this approach aligns with the expectations of a leader role from a particular lens, thus appealing to postsecondary leaders in a North American setting. To bring about the cultural shift needed to make postsecondary institutions more inclusive, the visionary and charismatic leadership qualities of a transformational leader are important. Another positive aspect of transformational leadership as it relates to change is that the leader is involved in shaping meaning in the organization. The challenge with this approach, as mentioned, is that it relies on the traits and personality of the leader, a tendency referred to as "heroic bias." This limits who can lead the change in the institution with respect to diversity and inclusive education. Although the transformational leadership approach seeks to build capacity in individuals and empower them, it does not appear to provide a space for leaders to "identify inequities and injustices that lead to the marginalization and exclusion of those who should be full participants in their organizations" (Shields, 2002, p. 219). Socioeconomic issues and power differentials appear to be glossed over in this approach.

Adaptive Leadership. I also drew on adaptive leadership theory, which focuses on "the adaptations required of people in response to changing environments" (Northouse, 2016, p. 257). Adaptive leadership concerns itself with encouraging and preparing individuals and organizations for change. It focuses on the activities that a leader needs to perform with the followers to effect change. Adaptive leadership has been characterized as leadership that helps other people explore and revise their values (Northouse, 2016). Adaptive leadership incorporates four viewpoints: a systems view, which acknowledges that the challenges people face are part of complex and interactive systems; a biological view, which acknowledges that people develop and evolve in response to the environment; a service orientation, whereby leaders use their skills and knowledge to serve others; and psychotherapy perspectives, whereby a supportive environment is put in place for changes to take place. Adaptive leadership is viewed as a process whereby "the behaviours of leaders encourage learning, creativity, and adaptation by followers in complex situations" (Northouse, 2016, p. 292).

The three major components of the model of adaptive leadership are situational challenges, leader behaviours, and adaptive work. When working through a challenge, leaders need to be able to view the big picture and then identify the type of situational challenges (technical, technical and adaptive, or adaptive) they seek to address. Adaptive challenges "usually require changes in people's assumptions, perceptions, beliefs, attitudes, and behaviors" (Northouse, 2016, p. 262). Change causes tension and distress in people. Regulating distress is a leadership behaviour in the adaptive leadership model that leaders need to perform. Resistance to change, especially change that relates to values and beliefs, is common; therefore, maintaining disciplined attention on the adaptive challenge and change that needs to occur is a required leadership behaviour. Allowing people to work on solving the adaptive challenges identified is the fifth leadership behaviour. Lastly, and perhaps most importantly, the adaptive leadership model stipulates that the leader listens to or encourages the expression of ideas from underrepresented or marginalized groups in the organization.

One strength of adaptive leadership is that it is a process approach that is follower centered. Additionally, it helps people "confront their personal values and adjust these as needed in order for change and adaptation to occur" (Northouse, 2016, p. 175). Furthermore, adaptive leadership is practical in that it provides ideas and suggestions on what leaders can do to make it work. Adaptive leadership encourages and prepares people for change. The model provides concrete activities that leaders can undertake to effect change. Through the creation of a safe space, it encourages people in the organization to challenge beliefs and assumptions, which is crucial when seeking to become inclusive of diverse populations in postsecondary institutions. In this approach, a safe space to challenge values and beliefs provides an opportunity for socioeconomic issues and power differentials to be considered. Marginalized groups or underrepresented voices can be "protected." Adaptive leadership considers that changes are a part of a complex system and cannot be compartmentalized to departments. This approach is not dependent on the character or traits of a leader. It calls for a relationship between all stakeholders.

Adaptive leadership does have weaknesses. Northouse (2016) pointed to the fact that it is a relatively new approach, and very little research has been done on it. Secondly, the relationship between factors described in the adaptive process is not clearly delineated. This model has a wide perspective range and can sometimes be abstract. Lastly, Northouse highlighted that adaptive leadership does not address a moral dimension, especially given that it involves mobilizing people to make changes related to values and beliefs. When seeking to bring about changes to beliefs, values, and assumptions, it is important to ask whose or which values the postsecondary institution is aspiring to and whether these changes are for societal benefit.

Social Justice Leadership. Social justice has been defined differently by scholars (e.g., Drago-Severson & Blum-DeStefano, 2017; Furman, 2012; Kowalchuk, 2019; Lopez, 2016; Lopez & Olan, 2018; Shah, 2018). According to Blackmore (2009, as cited in Furman, 2012), social justice "encompasses a range of terms – some more powerful than others – such as equity, equality, inequality, equal opportunity, affirmative action, and most recently diversity" (p. 193). Similarly, Drago-Severson and Blum-DeStefano (2017) declared that the term "social justice" is being employed as "a catch-all phrase" and refers to "anything and everything" related to diversity (p. 461). Though there is a lack of clarity with the definition and conceptualization of social justice, this concept "has deep roots and is driven by a commitment to highlighting, exploring, and addressing systemic prejudices and inequities through individual and collective action" (Drago-Severson & Blum DeStefano, 2017, p. 461). For some individuals, social justice is

> a way of looking at the world through a critical lens that highlights justice and injustice. To others it is a way of thinking about and practicing education and schooling that demands action that speaks the truth to power, rallies for freedom, liberates minds and bodies, wrests freedom from tyranny and emancipates thoughts and freedom. (Brooks, 2012, as cited in Lopez, 2016, p. 27)

Social justice leaders "make issues of race, class, gender, disability, sexual orientation, and other historically and currently marginalizing conditions" (Theoharis, 2007, as cited in Lopez, 2016, p. 7). Similarly, antiracism scholars such as George Sefa Dei, Carl James, and Malinda Smith make issues of these social difference markers. For Lopez (2016), social justice leadership is concerned with advocacy, challenging injustice, and leading change in order to better serve the needs of marginalized individuals (p. 28). The practices of social justice leaders include "conscious actions to bring about change in their schools by ensuring that the curriculum is reflective of all learners and students, whose experiences have traditionally been excluded, are included" (Lopez, 2017b, p. 27). Additionally, Lopez (2016) declared that social justice leaders engage in hiring practices that are aimed at increasing diversity in teaching staff by intentionally hiring teachers of color.

Kowalchuk (2019) expanded on the literature on social justice leadership practices by providing examples of how school leaders have engaged in these practices. In a qualitative study that was grounded in critical theory and conducted with school principals in Canada, Kowalchuk found five practices that principals engaged to address injustice and the marginalization of students. First, they demonstrated social justice. Demonstrating social justice entailed engaging colleagues in discussion on matters revolving around issues of injustice, being explicit in communicating a social justice vision, and modelling behaviours on how to be socially just. Second, they challenged the status quo, which meant questioning and critiquing the established power structure in the school. Third, they exercised critical instructional leadership, engaging teachers in "deconstructing the curriculum through a lens of cultural responsiveness and relevance" (Kowalchuk, 2019, Exercise Critical Instructional Leadership section, para. 2). Fourth, they shared and preserved respectful relationships. The principals in this study stressed the importance of ensuring respectful relationships between those who are marginalized and those that have power. Finally, they honoured "voice". Providing students, teachers, and the community with space to have their voices heard regarding school matters allowed for all stakeholders to feel respected and empowered. Honouring voice enables leaders to "acknowledge and distribute power equitably," (Kowalchuk, 2019, Honour Voice section, para. 5) thus, building capacity and empowerment.

Educators who engage in social justice leadership practices face challenges. In a study with Canadian school leaders in the K-12 system who sought to make curriculum changes more inclusive of diversity, Lopez (2016) revealed the challenges or "tensions" that these leaders experienced and drew attention to the following: facing resistance from colleagues, addressing the needs of the community, balancing personal and professional lives, building capacity and ongoing learning, and dealing with challenges of racism. These challenges can be viewed as occurring at personal and interpersonal levels of interaction.

Interpersonal challenges occur between leaders and other people with whom they interact such as colleagues in the school and members of the community the school serves. According to participants in the study, resistance stemmed from colleagues not being "ready to embrace change in critical ways that pushed boundaries" (Lopez, 2016, p. 51). One leader referred to how "it is easy to add samosas to the cuisine in the cafeteria but there is a reluctance to look at the Math or the History curriculum and create deep lasting change in instruction and materials" (Lopez, 2016, p. 51). Addressing the needs of the community requires the involvement of the diverse community of parents in decision-making processes. This creates tension in that some leaders "respond to the needs of the communities differently, often in ways that some are not used to doing" (Lopez, 2016, p. 52).

Lopez (2016) indicated that at a personal level, social justice work requires a significant time and emotional commitment from leaders. This creates a challenge for them in balancing their personal and professional lives in order to avoid becoming burnt out. Leaders in the study also expressed the importance of professional development to support their social justice leadership practices. Some leaders shared how they developed a deeper understanding of themselves and how "they themselves had internalized oppression, and had to navigate their own pain and impact on their practice" (Lopez, 2016, p. 57). They expressed the challenges of discussing racism in their schools when there was reluctance to engage in such a discussion. Lopez (2016) argued that "racism cannot be swept under the rug. These issues must be addressed in schools if students of color are to feel safe, valued and respected" (p. 55).

In exploring the preparedness of teacher candidates to teach a diverse student population, Lopez and Olan (2018) argued for the need for teacher candidates to appreciate diversity from a critical perspective if social justice in education is to be addressed. They observed that a challenge educators face in Canada is "how teacher educators theorize, engage with and understand diversity themselves" (Lopez & Olan, 2018, p. 164). For some teacher candidates, naming oppressive structures such as racism was a challenge as they did not feel comfortable doing so. Some teacher candidates felt they did not have the skills and competencies to name and address oppressive structures in their teaching practices. It is important to consider that some educational leaders may not engage in leadership practice from a critical perspective for similar reasons.

The studies conducted by Lopez (2016), Lopez and Olan (2018), and Kowalchuk (2019) indicated that social justice leadership practices occur both in concrete and abstract ways at various levels of interaction and organizational structure. Social justice leadership practices can be contemplated through the praxis-dimensions-capacities framework for social justice leadership (Furman, 2012). This conceptual framework encompasses three concepts with regard to social justice. First, social justice is seen as praxis. Furman (2012) defined praxis as

> the continual, dynamic interaction among knowledge acquisition, deep reflection, and action at two levels – the intrapersonal and the extrapersonal – with the purpose of transformation and liberation. At the intrapersonal level, praxis involves self-knowledge, critical self-reflection, and acting to transform oneself as a leader for social justice. At the extrapersonal level, praxis involves knowing and understanding systemic social justice issues, reflecting on these issues, and taking action to address them. (p. 203)

Second, social justice stretches over several dimensions wherein practice occurs. These dimensions are personal, interpersonal, communal, systemic, and ecological. Third, each dimension of social justice calls for certain specific capacities required of leaders (p. 202).

According to Furman's (2012) praxis-dimensions-capacities framework for social justice leadership, leaders in the personal dimension engage in "deep, critical, and honest self-reflection" (p. 205) in order to "explore their values, assumptions, and biases in regard to race, class, language, sexual orientation, and so on and in turn, how these affect their leadership practice" (p. 205). In the interpersonal dimension, leaders engage knowledge generated in the personal dimension to interact with others and build relationships. Furman stated that in this dimension, praxis "involves the leader's self-knowledge and reflection in regard to communication / interaction style and behaviors and how these affect and possibly contribute to silencing and marginalizing others" (2012, p. 207). In the communal dimension, leaders "work to build community across cultural groups through inclusive, democratic practices" (Furman, 2012, p. 209). Social justice leadership practices in the systemic dimension include leaders "assessing, critiquing, and working to transform the system, at the school and district levels, in the interest of social justice and learning for all" (Furman, 2012, p. 210). Last, social justice leadership practices in the ecological dimension include "acting with the knowledge that school-related social justice issues are situated within broader issues of oppression and sustainability" (p. 211).

Furthermore, praxis—knowledge, reflection, and action—requires that social justice leaders engage in the five dimensions using certain capacities and skills. In short, social justice leaders need to develop capacity and skills for self-transformation, relationship building, team building, communication and inclusion, transformative action, and skills to share and exchange knowledge on how the institution is situated in the broader societal context.

Drago-Severson and Blum-DeStefano (2017) explained that "a constructive-developmental lens can help us better understand how educators' internal capacities influence their teaching and leadership for social justice, as well as their orientations toward race, diversity, identity, privilege, and collaboration within and across lines of difference" (p. 460). In order for leaders to develop the capacities needed to engage in social justice leadership practices, it is important to understand their "qualitatively different ways of knowing – or developmental meaning making systems" (Drago-Severson & Blum-DeStefano, 2017, p. 457), which shape how they engage diversity and social justice issues.

From a constructive development theory perspective, adults use one of four ways to make sense of their experiences: instrumental, socializing, self-authoring, and self-transforming. Adults who use an instrumental way of knowing engage in social justice practice from "more concrete, transactional, and individualistic approaches" (Drago-Severson & Blum-DeStefano, 2017, p. 467). Drago-Severson and Blum-DeStefano (2017) pointed out that instrumental knowers pay attention to "more immediate surroundings and specific individuals rather than organizational or systemic dynamics" (p. 468). Adults who are socializing knowers "have the internal capacity to understand and consider others' experiences and perspectives" (Drago-Severson & Blum-DeStefano, 2017, p. 469), but they need validation and approval from those around them. Self-authoring knowers define their positionality. They "prioritize and integrate competing values, engage in necessary conflict without feeling torn apart, and think systematically about larger organizational and societal challenges and their roles in them" (Drago-Severson & Blum-DeStefano, 2017, p. 471). Last, self-transforming knowers "see that their identities and self-systems are, by definition, limited and that they need others not *to be complete* (like socializing knowers) but to *feel more complete*" (Drago-Severson & Blum-DeStefano, 2017, p. 472).

Upon reflection, I think that the type of self-reflection that occurs in the personal dimension through the various ways of knowing as described by Drago-Severson and Blum DeStefano (2017) matters for social justice leadership. In her work on culturally responsive and socially just leadership, Lopez (2016) insisted on the importance of critical reflection for leaders where they examine their personal histories, values, beliefs, and how they bring these to their roles. Additionally, the critical reflection must incorporate how these leaders' personal identities are perceived by students. I would extend this to include a critical self-reflection in the personal dimension that incorporates how leaders' identities are understood and experienced by other leaders as well as faculty and nonfaculty members in the institution. For Lopez (2016), culturally responsive leadership and social justice leadership are closely connected in that leaders who engage in these approaches challenge the various forms of oppression in educational settings. The main principles of culturally responsive leadership are as follows:

- the development of emancipatory consciousness that focuses on educators' awareness of the history and detrimental impact of social inequities;
- equitable insights that focus on the development of attitudes that promote inclusion throughout the school community; and
- engagement in reflexive practices whereby educators critically examine the work that they do. (Lopez, 2016, p. 19)

For educational leaders to engage in social justice leadership, they need to have what Lopez (2016) described as cultural competence and sociopolitical and critical consciousness.

Current dominant discourses on leadership are from Western European conceptualizations that are steeped in coloniality (Lopez, 2021) and that focus on the individual's skills and capabilities to inspire and organize community members (Dei, 2019; James, 2019). Lopez (2021) argued that educational leadership practices perpetuate colonial oppression and coloniality. In the field of education, coloniality includes power and control of knowledge and erasures of non-Western epistemologies (Lopez, 2021). According to James (2019), leadership from this dominant perspective is "conceived of as the capability and skills that individuals possess to identify the needs or assets of a group or community, and to inspire and mobilize others to join with them in addressing the needs or mobilizing the assets" (p. 22). Furthermore, the ways in which leaders exercise their power is "based on a value system informed by their social circumstances, lived experiences, and acquired ideologies – all of which mediate the integrity, humility, shared goals, and capacity to make tough decisions on which leadership roles are to be built" (James, 2019, p. 22). Leaders' ways of doing and being are neither neutral nor objective. James (2019) further explained that current ways of evaluating leadership are based on Western Eurocentric ways of knowing and understanding. Dei (2019) argued there is need to explore counter hegemonic conceptualizations of leadership.

Challenging the current and dominant Western Eurocentric approaches to leadership calls for critical leadership approaches such as decolonizing educational leadership. I take up decolonization as a process of undoing coloniality by dismantling the structures that uphold and maintain the power and dominance of a particular way of knowing and being over others (Lopez, 2021). The structures that uphold coloniality are reflected in the biases that Smith et al. (2017) described as canonical and curriculum biases, affinity bias and homosocial reproduction, resume racism, and accent bias among more. Dismantling these power structures calls for challenging systemic racism and white Eurocentric ways of knowing through leaders' engagement in self-reflexivity in relation to coloniality, critical dialogue, disruption of neoliberal educational policies, and building relationships across communities (Lopez, 2021).

In contrast to a Western Eurocentric approach, leadership from Indigenous and African perspectives is "less about individual attributes and skills than shared community expectations and roles. An African-centered / Indigenous perspective sees leadership as not about a romantic or charismatic persona. Leadership is not about the individual" (Dei, 2019, p. 354). The challenge with the dominant Western European conceptualizations is the lack of "critical engagement with equity, social justice, and diverse local and cultural knowings about leadership from the perspective of marginalized and oppressed communities" (Dei, 2019, p. 353). Leadership from Indigenous and African ways of knowing is spiritually informed, references the teachings of the Earth, and focuses on the community, not the individual. Power is distributed among community members. These approaches to leadership honour the contributions and participation of every voice in the community in consensual decision-making processes. According to Dei (2019), "it is a kind of leadership where everyone has something to contribute and participates in without being victimized" (p. 354).

James (2019) advocated for black leaders in Canada to act as cultural curators. Cultural curators are defined as "leaders who centre the culture of the community in their performance of leadership" (James, 2019, p. 37) and "play a significant role in voicing, and placing into 'mainstream' conversation, the concerns and perspectives of the Black communities, which invariably affect the social and cultural discourses of the communities and of society generally" (James, 2019, pp. 39–40). Dei (2019) challenged readers to reflect on the question: "Are there Indigenous, anti-colonial patterns of leadership we could be exploring and building to foster shared responsibility and meet social expectations?" (p. 353). Similarly, James (2019) called for a critical reflection "on the various approaches to leadership that account for the situation in which we find ourselves today, and with the purpose of doing activism differently in order to gain the needed social change" (p. 22).

From a black critical LGBTQ perspective, Crichlow (2019) indicated that "Black heteronormative leadership ... does not make space for LGBTQ persons to see ourselves as leaders or contribute to thinking about Black leadership" (p. 290). He further argued that the voices of black queers, gender nonconforming, and nonbinary persons are not included in black leadership. Exclusion of black LGBTQ activists also occurs in the broader LGBTQ community. Crichlow advocated for black leadership that does not replace "one form of heterocentric domination with another, and to accept new, intersectional cultural modes for educating, mobilizing, and organizing to achieve the best interests of the community" (2019, p. 305). Social justice leadership requires creating a space that meets the needs of all marginalized people.

The Integrated Social Justice Leadership Framework for Diversity and Inclusivity

After reading what other scholars have researched on diversity, inclusion, organizational culture, implicit bias, and leadership and after discussing these concepts with the nine leaders who participated in my study, I generated the integrated social justice leadership framework for diversity and inclusivity. This is a conceptual framework to understand how postsecondary leaders make meaning of diversity and inclusivity in educational settings. In this section, I share briefly how I arrived at my conceptual framework. I then describe the main concepts and subconcepts and how they are interconnected. I also discuss the significance of the integrated social justice leadership framework as a lens to think through how postsecondary leaders understand, interpret and enact values of diversity and inclusivity in educational settings.

At the beginning of my research, I identified diversity, inclusivity, organizational culture, and leadership as key interconnected concepts that informed my research questions. After meeting with the nine leaders, the relationships between the four concepts became more apparent. My field notes pointed to the need for me to revisit the literature and attend to insights participants shared with me that I had not considered prior to the interviews. In revisiting the literature, I identified social justice leadership and implicit bias as key concepts to understand how leaders make meaning of diversity and inclusivity in postsecondary educational settings. A critical review of the literature, coupled with insights from my field notes, contributed to the development of the integrated social justice leadership framework for diversity and inclusivity as visualized in Figure 2.1.

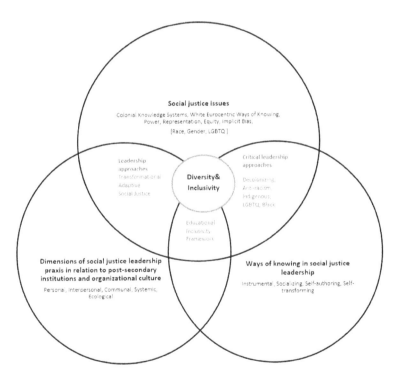

Figure 2.1. Integrated Social Justice Leadership Framework for Diversity and Inclusivity

The integrated social justice leadership framework for diversity and inclusivity provides a way to think through the epistemological positioning of leaders with regard to diversity and inclusivity within the varying dimensions in which they practice leadership and in which they attend to social justice issues in postsecondary settings. These are issues that reflect the context in which leadership is practiced. As described in Chapter 1, leaders are engaging in leadership practices in a context of increasing diversity in the student demographic and increasing demands from social justice movements calling for issues of race, gender, sexual orientation, and more to be addressed.

Source: Maroro Zinyemba

At the centre of the framework is the phenomenon of this inquiry: diversity and inclusivity. The literature shows that diversity and inclusivity are conceptualized differently among scholars (Ahmed, 2012; Castania 1996; Dei, 2000; DeLuca, 2013; Janssens & Steyaert, 2003; James, 2011b). In the integrated social justice leadership framework, I take up diversity as the social difference markers among people. Inclusivity refers to a state or setting where members of an organization are able to identify and connect with the organization's social environment, culture, population, and history. Each member of the organization has an equal voice and all members participate as equally important contributors and cocreators in all aspects of an organization (Dei & Asgharzadeh, 2017, p. 2).

I broach the dimensions of social justice leadership praxis in Furman's (2012) terms: personal, interpersonal, communal, systemic, and ecological. I place these dimensions in the context of organizational culture as defined by Wolfe and Dilworth (2015) as "a combination of values, beliefs, language, rituals, and ideologies that are explicit and implicit through day-to-day practices within an organization" (p. 671). Leadership praxis in postsecondary institutions occurs in the varying dimensions of practice as they relate to diversity and inclusivity, and these are situated in a particular organizational culture. Additionally, leadership praxis is drawn from different ways of knowing with regard to diversity and inclusivity.

In the integrated social justice leadership framework for diversity and inclusivity, I take up ways of knowing as described in constructive development theory (Drago-Severson & Blum-DeStefano, 2017). This framework provides a way to understand how these ways of knowing "influence our orientations toward diversity, difference, and teaching and leading for social justice" (Drago-Severson & Blum-DeStefano, 2017, p. 466). In the integrated social justice leadership framework for diversity and inclusivity, I recognize that, beginning with the personal dimension, adults come to know and make sense of diversity and inclusivity in their own ways. I take up the ways of knowing that adults engage in as instrumental, socializing, self-authoring, and self-transforming. I have thought through these four ways of knowing in order to gain a broad sense of the worldview of the participants and how they embrace diversity and inclusivity. Drago-Severson and Blum-DeStefano (2017) posited that through a constructive development lens, we "understand more about how people understand themselves, their work, and the world, we are better positioned to communicate and connect in ways that matter for social justice" (p. 464).

I draw from critical race and social justice scholars Dei (2000, 2001, 2014), Smith (2017, 2019), James (2011a, 2011b, 2017), Lopez (2016, 2021), St. Denis (2011), and Ahmed (2012) the social justice issues of colonial knowledge systems, white Eurocentric ways of knowing, power, representation, and implicit bias as they relate to social difference markers of race, gender, and LGBTQ identity. These are issues that postsecondary leaders navigate in institutions with a declared commitment to values of diversity and inclusivity. Social justice issues, dimensions of social justice leadership praxis in organizations, and ways of knowing in social justice leadership are interconnected. In the current postsecondary context, leaders are confronted with social justice issues as they relate to diversity and inclusivity in educational settings. They operate in a particular organizational culture where diversity and inclusivity have been publicly declared as values to which leaders are committed. Within a particular organizational culture, leaders engage in praxis in varying dimensions beginning with the personal. The way in which leaders approach diversity and inclusivity is informed by their ways of knowing.

Within this interconnectedness are subconcepts, which are discourses on leadership and the framework for educational inclusivity. I explored three approaches to leadership related to change: transformational leadership, adaptive leadership, and social justice leadership. These three approaches are actualized within the dimensions of praxis and they draw from ways of knowing diversity and inclusivity. Leaders who engage in social justice leadership, for example, draw from one of the four ways of knowing and engage in the various dimensions of practice within their organization and culture. I also explored critical leadership perspectives: Indigenous and Afrocentric leadership (Dei, 2019), black leadership (James, 2019), and black and LGBTQ (Crichlow, 2019) leadership. These three approaches are directly informed by social justice issues and seek ways to address them. They account for the multiple and intersecting identities of individuals. According to Dei (2000), "these identities are also sites of shifting power relations that inform, constrain and determine the human experience and condition" (p. 31). These are leadership perspectives that draw from ways of knowing and invite critiques of dominant leadership perspectives as they relate to diversity and inclusivity.

The interdisciplinary framework for educational inclusivity as framed by DeLuca (2013) broaches four conceptions of diversity and inclusivity and sets them along a continuum. I offer the view that this continuum exists within an organizational culture where issues of social justice are taken up and leadership praxis occurs in the varying dimensions. In the interdisciplinary framework, issues of power are not always considered hierarchical. I offer that how leaders approach power relations along the continuum is influenced by their ways of knowing.

Conclusion

The literature review presented varying definitions and conceptualizations of diversity. Diversity has been defined through visible dimensions such as race, gender, and ethnicity as well as invisible dimensions such as socioeconomic status and education level. Some scholars argue that sociohistorical context and power should inform the conceptualization of diversity given that diversity involves intergroup relations. Conceptualizing diversity as the differences among people with respect to social difference markers and through a questioning of power relations resonates with me.

As the demographic makeup of the student body on postsecondary campuses becomes increasingly diverse, the need for recognition of diversity and inclusivity in education has become even more urgent. Research shows that a diverse faculty and staff positively influences the success rate of students from underrepresented groups. Some postsecondary institutions have embarked on diversity planning programs with an aim to increase faculty diversity and to influence institutional policy and practice. Studies show that organizational cultural changes are necessary for successful diversity planning. Leadership is instrumental in implementing any sort of organizational cultural change. However, there are varying conceptualizations of leadership.

To gain an understanding of how postsecondary leaders make meaning of diversity and inclusivity in educational settings, I developed the integrated social justice leadership framework for diversity and inclusivity, which is underpinned by three theoretical frameworks: the ways of knowing with which leaders approach the phenomenon of diversity and inclusivity; social justice issues of colonial knowledge systems, white Eurocentric ways of knowing, power, representation, and implicit bias as they relate to the social difference markers of race, gender, and sexual orientation; and dimensions in which social justice leadership praxis occur.

References

Aguirre, A., & Martinez, R. (2002). Leadership practices and diversity in higher education: Transitional and transformational frameworks. *The Journal of Leadership Studies*, 8(3), 53–62. https://doi.org/10.1177/107179190200800305

Ahmed, S. (2012). On being included: Racism and diversity in institutional life. Duke University Press.

Alberta Education. (n.d.). Inclusive education. https://www.alberta.ca/inclusive-education.aspx

Alberta School Councils' Association. (2019). Principles of inclusive education. https://www.albertaschoolcouncils.ca/education-in-alberta/alberta-education-initiatives/principles-of-inclusion

Burke, L. (2013). Why we can't wait: Diversity planning in community colleges. Community College Journal of Research and Practice, 37(11), 839–843. https://doi.org/10.1080/10668921003744934

Castania, K. (1996). What is diversity? Cornell University Cooperative Extension. https://extension.usu.edu/employee/files/newletters/diversity704.pdf

Crichlow, W. (2019). Black consciousness and the heteronormative sexual politics of Black leadership in Toronto: A commentary. In T. Kitossa, E. S. Lason, & P. S. S. Howard (Eds.), *African Canadian Leadership* (pp. 345–369). University of Toronto Press. https://doi.org/10.3138/9781487531409

Dei, G. (2000). Towards an Anti-racism discursive framework. In G. S. Dei & A. Calliste (Eds.), *Power, knowledge and anti-racist education* (pp. 23–40). Fernwood Publishing.

Dei, G. (2001). Rescuing theory: Anti-racism and inclusive education. *Race, Gender & Class*, 8(1), 139–161. https://www.jstor.org/stable/41674965

Dei, G. J. (2014). Personal reflections on anti-racism education for a global context. *Encounters on Education*, 15, 239–249.

Dei, G. J. S. (2019). An Indigenous Africentric perspective on Black leadership. In T. Kitossa, E. S. Lason, & P. S. S. Howard (Eds.), *African Canadian leadership* (pp. 345–369). University of Toronto Press. https://doi.org/10.3138/9781487531409

Dei, G. J. S., & Asgharzadeh, A. (2017). Inclusive education and social development in an African context. *Comparative and International Education Society of Canada*, 33(2), 2–16. https://doi.org/10.5206/cie-eci.v33i2.9041

Dei, G. J. S., James, I. M., Karumanchery, L. L, James-Wilson, S., & Zine, J. (2000). *Removing the margins: The challenges and possibilities of inclusive schooling*. Canadian Scholars' Press.

DeLuca, C. (2013). Toward an interdisciplinary framework for educational inclusivity. Canadian Journal of Education, 36(1), 305–348.

Dimmock, C., & Walker, A. (2005). Educational leadership culture and diversity. Sage Publications.

Drago-Severson, E., & Blum-DeStefano, J. (2017). The self in social justice: A developmental lens on race, identity, and transformation. *Harvard Educational Review*, 87(4), 457–481.

Elam, C., & Brown, G. (2005). The inclusive university: Helping minority students choose a college and identify institutions that value diversity. Journal of College Admission, 187, 14–17.

Furman, G. (2012). Social justice leadership as praxis: Developing capacities through preparation programs. *Educational Administration Quarterly*, 48(2), 191–229. https://doi.org/10.1177/0013161X11427394

Hughes, B. (2015). Recruiting, retaining, and benefiting from a diverse community college faculty: A case study of one college's successes. Community College Journal of Research and Practice, 39(7), 659–672. https://doi.org/10.1080/10668926.2014.885401

James, C. E. (2011a, May 15). Canada: Paradoxes of 'visible minorities' in job ads. University World News. https://www.universityworldnews.com/post.php?story=20110513185935314

James, C. E. (2011b, December 2). Isn't it about time we admit race matters? EdCan Network. https://www.edcan.ca/articles/isnt-it-about-time-we-admit-that-race-matters/

James, C. E. (2011c). Multicultural education in a color-blind society. In C.A. Grant & A. Portera (Eds.), Intercultural and multicultural education: Enhancing global interconnectedness (pp. 191–210). Taylor and Francis. https://doi.org/10.4324/9780203848586

James, C. E. (2017). "You know why you were hired, don't you?": Expectations and challenges in university appointments. In F. Henry, E. Dua, C. E. James, A. Kobayashi, P. Li, H. Ramos, & M. S. Smith (Eds.), The equity myth: Racialization and indigeneity at Canadian Universities (pp. 155–170). University of British Columbia Press.

James, C. E. (2019). Black leadership and white logic: Models of community engagement. In T. Kitossa, E. S. Lason, & P. S. S. Howard (Eds.), *African Canadian leadership* (pp. 345–369). University of Toronto Press. https://doi.org/10.3138/9781487531409

James, C. E., & Chapman-Nyaho, S. (2017). "Would never be hired these days": The precarious work situation of racialized and Indigenous faculty members. In F. Henry, E. Dua, C. E. James, A. Kobayashi, P. Li, H. Ramos, & M. S. Smith (Eds.), The equity myth: Racialization and indigeneity at Canadian Universities (pp. 84–114). University of British Columbia Press.

Janssens, M., & Steyaert, C. (2003). Theories of diversity within organisation studies: Debates and future trajectories. SSRN Electronic Journal. https://doi.org/10.2139/ssrn.389044

Jeffcoat, K., & Piland, W. E. (2012). Anatomy of a community college faculty diversity program. Community College Journal of Research and Practice, 36(6), 397–410. https://doi.org/10.1080/10668920902813477

Kouzes, J. M., & Posner, B. Z. (2012). The leadership challenge: How to make extraordinary things happen in organizations (5th ed.). Jossey-Bass.

Kowalchuk, D. (2019). Voices for change: Social justice leadership practices. *Journal of Educational Leadership and Policy Studies*, 3(1). https://files.eric.ed.gov/fulltext/EJ1226 940.pdf

Lopez, A. E. (2016). *Culturally responsive and socially just leadership: From theory to action.* Palgrave MacMillan

Lopez, A. E. (2017a). Is it time for a sixth dimension of multicultural education?: Resistance and praxis in challenging times. Multicultural Perspectives, 19(3), 155–161. https://doi. org/10.1080/15210960.2017.1331740

Lopez, A. E. (2017b). Rocky boats and rainbows: Culturally responsive leadership from the margin – An autoethnography. In A. Esmail, A. Pitre, & A. Aragon (Eds.), *Perspectives on diversity, equity, and social justice in educational leadership* (pp. 23–40). Rowman & Littlefield.

Lopez, A. E. (2020). Reflection: Harnessing energy of social movements for lasting change. *Multicultural Perspectives*, 22(3), 115–117. https://doi.org/10.1080/15210 960.2020.1794467

Lopez. A. E. (2021). Examining alternative school leadership practices and approaches: A decolonising school leadership approach. *Intercultural Education*. https://doi.org/10.1080/14675 986.2021.1889471

Lopez, A. E., & Olan, E. L. (2018). *Transformative pedagogies for teacher education: Moving towards critical praxis in an era of change.* Information Age Publishing.

Loreman, T. (2007). Seven pillars of support for inclusive education: Moving from "Why?" to "How? International Journal of Whole Schooling, 3(2), 22–38.

Loreman, T. (2014). Measuring inclusive education outcomes in Alberta, Canada. International Journal of Inclusive Education, 18(5), 459–483.

Northouse, P. (2016). *Leadership: Theory and practice.* Sage Publications.

Ryan, J. (2002). Leadership in contexts of diversity and accountability. In K. Leithwood (Ed.), Second international handbook of educational leadership and administration (pp. 979–1001). Kluwer Academic Publishers.

Shah, V. (2018). Leadership for social justice through the lens of self-identified, racially and other-privileged leaders. *Journal of Global Citizenship and Equity Education*, 6(1), 1–41.

Sherman Garr, S., Shellenback, S., & Scales, J. (2014). Diversity and inclusion in Canada: The current state. Deloitte Development LLC. https://www2.deloitte.com/ca/en/pages/human-capital/articles/the-current-state-of-diversity-and-inclusion.html

Shields, C. M. (2002). Cross-cultural leadership and communities of difference: Thinking about leading diverse schools. In K. Leithwood (Ed.), Second international handbook of educational leadership and administration (pp. 209–224). Kluwer Academic Publishers.

Shohat, E., & Stam, R. (2014). Unthinking Eurocentrism : Multiculturalism and the media. Routledge

Smith, M. (2017). Disciplinary silences: Race, Indigeneity, and gender in the social sciences. In F. Henry, E. Dua, C. E. James, A. Kobayashi, P. Li, H. Ramos, & M. S. Smith (Eds.), The equity myth: Racialization and indigeneity at Canadian Universities (pp. 239–262). University of British Columbia Press.

Smith, M. (2019). *The diversity gap in 2019: Canadian U15 universities – Leadership pipeline.* Academic Women's Association, University of Alberta. https://uofaawa.files.wordpress.com/2019/06/2019_u15_leadership_diversity_gap_release_20jun2019_final-1.pdf

Smith, M., Gamarro, K., & Toor, M. (2017). A dirty dozen: Unconscious race and gender biases in the academy. In F. Henry, E. Dua, C. E. James, A. Kobayashi, P. Li, H. Ramos, & M. S. Smith (Eds.), The equity myth: Racialization and indigeneity at Canadian Universities (pp. 263–296). University of British Columbia Press.

St. Denis, V. (2011). Silencing Aboriginal curricular content and perspectives through multiculturalism: "There are other children here". *Review of Education, Pedagogy, and Cultural Studies, 33*(4), 306–317. https://doi.org/10.1080/10714413.2011.597638

Stout, R., Archie, C., Cross, D., & Carman, C. (2018). The relationship between faculty diversity and graduation rates in higher education. Intercultural Education, 29(3), 399–417.

Walker, A., & Dimmock, C. (2002). Moving school leadership beyond its narrow boundaries: Developing a cross-cultural approach. In K. Leithwood (Ed.), Second international handbook of educational leadership and administration (pp. 167–202). Kluwer Academic Publishers.

Walker, A., & Riordan, G. (2010). Leading collective capacity in culturally diverse schools. School Leadership & Management, 30(1), 51–63. https://doi.org/10.1080/13632430903509766

Williamson, W. J., & Gilham, C. (2014). Inclusion's Confusion in Alberta. International Journal of Inclusive Education, 18(6), 553–566. https://doi.org/10.1080/13603116.2013.802025

Wolfe, B. L., & Dilworth, P. (2015). Transitioning normalcy: Organizational culture, African American administrators, and diversity leadership in higher education. Review of Educational Research, 85(4), 667–697. https://doi.org/10.3102/0034654314565667

Zembylas, M., & Iasonos, S. (2010). Leadership styles and multicultural education approaches: An exploration of their relationship. International Journal of Leadership in Education, 13(2), 163–183. https://doi.org/10.1080/13603120903386969

DRAWING ON PERSONAL SOCIOHISTORICAL EXPERIENCES AND NAVIGATING IMPLICIT BIAS

Introduction

Nine postsecondary leaders from three institutions in the Canadian province of Alberta participated in my research study on diversity and inclusivity. My conversation with each leader focused on understanding how their perceptions of diversity shape their institution's culture of inclusivity and impact enactments in practice; how their understanding of their institution's culture of inclusivity informs their conceptualizations of diversity; and how they experience diversity and inclusivity in their organizations and how these experiences inform their conceptualizations of diversity and inclusivity. I shared profiles of these leaders along with their conceptualizations of diversity and inclusivity in Chapter 1. I invited the leaders to an interview to which they brought with them some documents and artifacts. The artifacts were photographs or images that captured how the leaders make meaning of diversity and inclusivity in postsecondary settings. Engaging the leaders in conversation on these images and photographs enabled them to share their perceptions and understanding of diversity and inclusivity. Leaders described and explained the documents and images during the interviews. Short descriptions of the artifacts are included in the participant profile description in Chapter 1 of this book.

In this and the following chapters I share the knowledge generated with the leaders on the phenomenon of diversity and inclusivity. The themes that emerged from this study reveal that to make meaning of diversity and inclusivity, leaders engage as follows: leaders draw on personal sociohistorical experiences; leaders navigate bias; leaders engage their institution's strategic direction on diversity and inclusivity; leaders encounter issues of representational diversity; and leaders situate diversity and inclusivity issues in the provincial sociopolitical context. To interpret the meaning of these themes, I engage the integrated social justice leadership framework for diversity and inclusivity.

Integrated Social Justice Leadership Framework for Diversity and Inclusivity

The integrated social justice leadership framework for diversity and inclusivity provides a way to think through how leaders in this study understand diversity and inclusivity within the varying dimensions in which they practice leadership in postsecondary settings as illustrated in Figure 3.1.

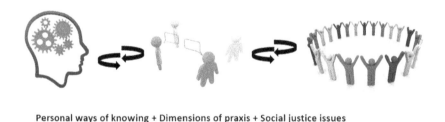

Personal ways of knowing + Dimensions of praxis + Social justice issues
(Drago-Severson & Blum DeStefano, 2017)   (Furman, 2012)   (Dei, Smith, James, Lopez, Ahmed, St. Denis)

Figure 3.1. Visualization: Integrated Social Justice Leadership Framework for Diversity and Inclusivity
Source: Maroro Zinyemba

Leaders in this inquiry shared their definitions of the phenomenon and though collectively they provided broad definitions of diversity, their conceptualizations of diversity and inclusivity largely centered on social difference markers of race, gender, and sexual orientation. The social justice issues that arose from the discussions on these social difference markers focused on issues of representation, implicit bias, and power. The themes show that leaders work through these social justice issues at various levels or dimensions, which are personal, interpersonal, communal, systemic, and ecological. Leaders make sense of diversity and inclusivity within these dimensions by engaging one or more of four ways of knowing, which are instrumental, socializing, self-authoring, and self-transforming. In short, instrumental knowers require concrete and clearly defined approaches to work through social justice issues. Socializing knowers consider the perspectives of and require validation from those around them when working through social justice concerns. Self-authoring knowers are able to see the role they play in societal challenges. Lastly, self-transforming knowers recognize there are multiple perspectives and realities that are equally important (Drago-Severson & Blum DeStefano, 2017).

In thinking through the themes in relation to the integrated social justice leadership framework for diversity and inclusivity, I found that, in the personal dimension, some leaders in this study engaged in critical self-reflection and explored their implicit biases about diversity and inclusivity using one of the following ways of knowing: socializing, self-authoring, and self-transforming. According to Furman (2012), praxis in the personal dimension "involves deep, critical, and honest self-reflection.... [Leaders] explore their values, assumptions, and biases ... [and] how these affect their leadership practice" (p. 205). Engaging in self-reflection and their relative position of power is important for leaders in antiracism work (Dei, 2000; Lopez & Olan, 2018). How leaders orient to diversity and inclusivity is important for understanding the expectations and actions of leaders in the various dimensions of social justice leadership practice.

The leaders in this inquiry shared their perceptions of the interpersonal interactions they have engaged in related to diversity and inclusivity with other individuals in postsecondary contexts who have their own ways of knowing. In this interpersonal dimension, praxis "first involves the leader's self-knowledge and reflection in regard to communication/interaction style and behaviors and how these affect and possibly contribute to silencing and marginalizing others" (Furman, 2012, p. 207). Interacting with other individuals using their own ways of knowing extends beyond the interpersonal level to the communal dimension. It is in the communal dimension that leaders continue to engage their ways of knowing and "work to build community across cultural groups through inclusive, democratic practices" (Furman, 2012, p. 207).

In the systemic dimension, leaders engage their personal sociohistorical experiences, ways of knowing, experiences, and knowledge from the interpersonal and communal dimensions for "assessing, critiquing, and working to transform the system" (Furman, 2012, p. 210) at the institutional level, which is the systemic dimension. From a critical race and social justice perspective, I found that it is in this dimension, in particular, that leaders engaging in social justice practices consider issues of representation, power, and implicit bias. They consider "institutional practices to see how institutions respond to the change of diversity and difference: understood as the intersections of race, gender, class, sexuality, language, culture and religion" (Dei, 2000, p. 34).

Finally, leaders in this study reflected on and shared their knowledge about postsecondary institutions' diversity and inclusivity in the Albertan sociopolitical context. According to the dimensions of social justice leadership practice, the Albertan sociopolitical context is considered as the ecological dimension. Leaders engage one of the four ways of knowing diversity and inclusivity as they work through public policy and interact with members of the public.

In this chapter, I present two themes: leaders draw on personal sociohistorical experiences and leaders navigate implicit bias to make meaning of the phenomenon. I then interpret these themes through the integrated social justice leadership framework for diversity and inclusivity, a framework that provides a lens through which we can understand how leaders understand and enact the phenomenon in their leadership practice.

Theme 1. Leaders Draw on Personal Sociohistorical Experiences

For some leaders, their background, experiences, and understanding of the self in relation to diversity are in alignment with the institution's position on inclusivity. These leaders' actions are informed by the institutional direction. Alex and Michelle shared this sense of alignment. Alex disclosed: "I've made intentional choices to work in a postsecondary that is about diversity and inclusion, and a lot of that stems from the things that I saw happen to my brother in our childhood." In addition, living among Indigenous Peoples in the Yukon influenced Alex's conceptualization of diversity and inclusivity. She stated, "I think the other thing, living remotely in the Yukon and with large Indigenous populations, that that was another part of my experience that has influenced how I see diversity too, because living there was a very inclusive society." Similarly, Michelle revealed, "I felt when I started working here that my attitudes matched up with what was happening… So, I feel like there was good synergy between what's happening at the institution and what was happening in my own life." Renee disclosed her personal sociohistorical experiences being married to somebody of a different race: "My spouse is of a different race than me…. We've been together for a long time. I've had the opportunity to see his experiences in the world." Having a sister identify as lesbian has also resulted in a shift for her. She shared,

> Having grown up in a small community, in a faith-based family, that [identifying as lesbian] was not, not okay. And so here was my sister who I loved and admired and wanting to be so much like who was telling me this. It took time for me to grapple with all of the things I'd been taught and the love I had for her. And so, for me that has been really instrumental, I think, in being a lot more open and accepting as well.

Paradoxically, for other leaders, such as Marlen and RNH, their background, experiences, and understanding of the self in relation to diversity are not aligned with the institutional positioning on inclusivity. RNH clearly stated, "Not yet, I would say" in discussing the alignment with his institution. He attributed this dissonance to his upbringing:

> And for me, I was just raised that way that you should really … everyone brings something to the table of value. And so, I was raised with that kind of openness, and then when I started learning and getting into leadership roles, I looked at my learning, my textbooks, my experience, through that different lens.

Interestingly, Marlen felt:

> Being a woman, being a child of immigrants, you know, being someone who straddles multiple religious spheres and being a woman of colour, there are a lot of components that I brought to the role, to the department, and therefore to the psyche of the institution through the initiatives and events that I did based off what I understood to be things that needed to be addressed.

For Marlen, her actions as a leader reflect her conceptualization of what diversity and inclusivity entail, and what she deems necessary for inclusivity. She sees the activities aimed at diversity and inclusivity in the institution as limited in scope and depth. She shared the following:

And I was putting things out there based off of what I was seeing in social media, current events, my own kind of pieces of advocacy I wanted to throw out there but it wasn't, "What does the institution teach first and foremost?" Embedding a culture of curiosity, embedding a culture of communal inquiry to understand what are the needs of the demographics you're serving in the first place rather than, "This is how we have defined, engaged with, and will deliver diversity and inclusion on campus."

Theme 2. Leaders Navigate Implicit Bias

To varying extents, leaders are aware that they have unconscious bias or implicit bias. Orla and Marlen acknowledged their levels of awareness of their assumptions. During the interview, Orla had an insight:

I am realizing as we talk that we are talking about diversity and inclusivity and I am doing the best that I can and I might have blinders on because that's natural. I have done some intercultural training and one of the big key things is the more you read and the more you think is the more you realize how biased you are and that kind of thing.

Marlen shared how she had noticed that she was an able-bodied person, something she had not considered in terms of inclusivity:

Being a fully able person over a couple of years in the role, I realized I was missing a big component that I needed to integrate. I think diversity and inclusion, I'm sure as cliche as it sounds, definitely starts with self-reflection.

Stella, Renee, and Orla shared their knowledge and perspectives on the activities taking place at an institutional level designed to raise awareness of implicit bias and the experiences of students of underrepresented groups. Renee shared that at an institutional level there is an awareness that more needs to be done to address unconscious bias and its effects. She stated:

I would say the institution is trying, we're doing a good job. There's still way more to do of course. And so, I think there's an awareness and understanding that it's not like we've got it and okay, we can stop the focus of this. Like there's a lot more to do for sure. But the desire to do more and to do better is definitely there.

Providing professional development opportunities for faculty and staff to raise awareness of unconscious bias and to provide ways to navigate it is a strategy that has been employed by institutions. Stella shared the following:

We have been working towards the development of a course for the college that everyone will have to take about Indigenous ways of being, knowing, and doing that I think will help shift that conversation and understanding. In my area we are developing a PD [professional development] offering for faculty on antiracism and inclusive pedagogy.

Similarly, Renee shared the learning opportunities provided at her institution that created a space for self-reflection. She stated:

We had a series of six sharing circles where we had elders and students and community members come and talk with us. And we really shared really openly and honestly amongst the team, our experiences, our understanding [of] Indigenous Peoples and learned an awful lot and had a lot of opportunity to reflect together as a group about it.

These efforts at an institutional level have increased awareness in some individuals. As a result of the sharing circles, said Renee, the outcome "has been that Indigenous students now feel safer coming to access services from student life because they see there's been a genuine desire to know and to learn more and consideration of indigenous ways of knowing into our practices."

Orla described her appreciation of such efforts at a professional development session that would cover information that some instructors lacked:

And I remember this was several years ago a particular instructor was there and I was like "I am so glad you are in this room right now" because, you know, he [an instructor participating in the professional development session] did not know what cisgender meant, you know things like that.

Knowing that they have implicit bias, leaders like Orla make efforts to monitor their assumptions when making decisions. For example, during the recruitment and hiring process for new faculty, Orla shared the strategy she uses to help mitigate her bias: "I always do think about that when I am recruiting. To not just gravitate to people who are like me. And by 'like me,' that might be white, that might also be style, you know." She said she makes an effort

to remember that each person is an individual person and if I see a name that suggests that they are from Country A, don't just automatically assume that they are going to sit there and do all these things, right? It's just a challenge to be aware of biases and experiences.

Such leaders also seek out professional development opportunities to engage with peers in order to create, exchange, and increase their knowledge on mitigating unconscious bias. Other leaders create professional development courses for faculty and staff to take.

Not all leaders are aware of their implicit bias. Some leaders who are actively engaged in diversity and inclusion efforts in their institutions state that implicit bias that their counterparts carry present a challenge in implementing inclusionary practices. Stella shared her perspective on the challenge presented by implicit bias: "I don't think that everyone who is in a leadership position understands that the systems and structures and processes are a particular value-based structure." She further stated,

> Having them [senior leaders] recognize that they are using a particular lens, like that's the biggest gap to me. They don't realize that there is a lens. That there is a lens they are using that is from a particular place. And that their lens is not the neutral lens. It's one of many lenses.

Alex believes that the homogeneity of the current faculty presents a limitation in terms of awareness of the needs of diverse students:

> We're hiring people who have gone to school here, their families put them through university, they've gone and got a Master's or a PhD, maybe they don't have any life experience. Maybe they've just come right here into the program to work, and so their view of the world is so different than our students' view of the world.

Because of her personal sociohistorical experiences, Alex finds "working with faculty who are very sheltered, or they just think that everybody is buying a house and having a baby and retiring on track, the same way that they are, to me it can be frustrating."

The image provided by Alex was that of a bookshelf, which captures the challenges that implicit bias may present. There were several shelves on this bookshelf each holding a variety of books. The books varied in size and their covers were of various colours. Not all the books were neatly ordered and arranged. Some books were tucked above other books. There were other objects on the bookshelf as well that were not books. In discussing the bookshelf image, Alex mentioned that some faculty and staff would be bothered by the toy on the bookshelf and the books that are not neatly arranged. She stated, "I know other people who ... would want to fix it, like that's something to be fixed." Their natural response would be to remove the toy mouse and to neatly arrange the untidy books. However, Alex advocated for faculty to "go into things with eyes wide and have good, basic understanding, but willingness to learn, willingness to not know, willingness not to think, 'I have to put all those books in order on that shelf.'" As a leader, Alex said her role with faculty who are not aware of their biases is to "invite the conversation by sharing stories, or being curious and asking questions that maybe will push them a bit outside of their worldview, so that they can challenge their thinking." Like Alex, Stella envisions a postsecondary setting where there is an awareness, appreciation, and inclusion of diversity. Stella's image of the tree trunk and tangled roots reflects this vision. In describing her picture, she shared,

> It's important that we become tangled from a diversity and equity and inclusion perspective in that I would like to see from when I look at this picture of all these roots is that instead of how I think it is now, which is Western European ways of being, knowing, and doing are the trunk and maybe everybody else gets to be a tiny tap root at the end.

Mitigating implicit bias requires challenging assumptions and causes discomfort for some. Stella and Marlen shared how this process is not easy. Marlen stated, "We can't espouse certain values until we understand the blind spots that we have because at some point we are not espousing all values. I think it's about challenging people…. It is about making people uncomfortable."

Stella said "it's about structural systemic change. And that is the part that I think is the hardest work." Both these leaders shared their struggles in challenging implicit bias that individuals carry. Stella referenced a book that she has used to help her navigate the sensitivities and challenges in raising awareness of bias. She shared that the book

> Gives concrete examples of what those concepts mean and how you can speak to people who have privilege about it in a way that isn't shutting them off and that doesn't shut me down. I get really passionate about these things and when people are frustrating, I need a guide to be able to help me articulate without offending.

Marlen has facilitated several workshops on implicit bias that have resulted in tension among participants. Nevertheless, she maintains that self-reflection is an important component of raising awareness of unconscious bias. She said,

> I think sometimes it's just going back to core basics of the Johari window. What do you know about yourself? What do you feel? Let us know about you. Going back to basic thinking. And I think that's how we can make diversity and inclusion digestible for other people… is making it a self-awareness practice … and this is what I do in my training all the time.

Leaders' level of awareness of their own implicit bias impacts the implementation of inclusionary practices and policies in the institution. Previous themes indicate that the strategic plan plays an integral role in creating a culture of inclusivity. A question that arises for me is the extent to which those articulating the strategic plan are aware of their own assumptions. It is worth considering the extent to which the structural and system changes that Marlen and Stella advocate can be brought about from the grassroots—that is, the student demographic, which is considerably more diverse than faculty and staff. I engage the integrated social justice leadership framework to interpret the themes and come to understand how postsecondary leaders in this inquiry make meaning of diversity and inclusivity.

Interpreting Personal Sociohistorical Experiences and Implicit Bias

> Being a woman, being a child of immigrants, you know, being someone who straddles multiple religious spheres and being a woman of colour, there are a lot of components that I brought to the role. (Marlen)

Understanding how postsecondary leaders' perceptions of diversity shape the institution's culture of inclusivity calls for an understanding of how leaders embody diversity and inclusivity and an understanding of their implicit biases or frames of reference. Marlen's quotation above demonstrates what Dei (2000) described as the interconnectedness of social differences. Leaders bring to their roles multiple identities which are "also sites of shifting power relations that inform, constrain and determine the human experience and condition" (Dei, 2000, p. 31). The themes show that leaders draw on personal sociohistorical experiences, which are informed by their multiple and intersecting identities, to make meaning of diversity and inclusivity in postsecondary contexts. It appears that what motivates leader engagement with inclusivity activities is the degree of alignment between a leader's personal sociohistorical experiences and the statements or commitments to diversity and inclusivity of their institutions.

According to the integrated social justice leadership framework for diversity and inclusivity, in the personal dimension, leaders "explore their values, assumptions, and biases in regard to race, class, language, sexual orientation, and so on and in turn how these affect their leadership practice" (Furman,

2012, p. 205). In exploring these assumptions, leaders engage in unique ways of knowing to make meaning of their context. Although in this study I did not set out to learn specifically about the diverse ways of knowing that leaders engage, it became apparent to me that some leaders presented self-authoring ways of knowing in the various dimensions of leadership praxis. These leaders shared how they "think systematically about larger organizational and societal challenges and their roles in them" (Drago-Severson & Blum DeStefano, 2017, p. 471). Other leaders presented self-transforming ways of knowing. Such leaders shared how they "see that their identities and self-systems are, by definition, limited and that they need others ... to *feel more complete*" (Drago-Severson & Blum DeStefano, 2017, p. 472). Leaders with self-authoring and self-transforming ways of knowing provided me with insight into how they embody diversity and inclusivity and understand their implicit biases.

Personal sociohistorical experiences. Scholars Janssens and Steyaert (2003) stressed that in order to understand diversity in a workplace context, it is imperative to consider the sociohistorical context. In this study, the themes show that for some leaders, there is an alignment between their conceptualization of diversity and their institution's statements and actions on inclusivity. It appears this alignment stems from their personal sociohistorical experiences with and orientation to diversity. For example, Alex, a program chair, shared that she intentionally chose to work at a postsecondary institution that valued diversity and inclusivity because of her personal experiences growing up with a brother who had a disability and her experiences living in Indigenous communities in the Yukon. Another program chair, Michelle, shared similar sentiments. For Renee, a vice president, being married to somebody of a different race and having a sister who identifies as a lesbian resulted in experiences that allow her to be "a lot more open and accepting as well" in her approach to inclusivity in the communal and systemic dimensions at her institution.

Leaders for whom an alignment exists between their personal sociohistorical experiences and the institution's position on inclusivity appear to engage in transformational leadership practices. For leaders such as Alex and Renee, this alignment motivates practices that promote inclusivity as defined by the institution. In the model of transformational leadership developed by Kouzes and Posner (2012), the five practices that transformational leaders perform are to model the way, inspire a shared vision, challenge the process, evolve others to act, and encourage the heart. Northouse (2016) added that transformational leaders are social architects in that "they make clear the emerging values and norms of the organization and help shape its meaning" (p. 176).

Alex, for example, inspires a vision of inclusivity in the department she leads by modelling the way through dialogue with faculty members. In describing the bookshelf image that she shared, Alex stated that her role as a leader has been to "invite the conversation by sharing stories, or being curious and asking questions that maybe will push them [faculty] a bit outside of their worldview, so that they can challenge their thinking." A closer look at the practices leaders like Alex engage suggests that such leaders are self-authoring knowers. These leaders "consider others' expectations, assessments, and suggestions in relation to their own bench of judgement" (Drago-Severson & Blum-DeStefano, 2017, p. 464). Such leaders are aware of their own implicit biases, societal challenges with regard to diversity and inclusivity, and the roles they play in advancing inclusivity in their institutions.

Interestingly, not all leaders in this study experience an alignment between their conceptualization of diversity and their institution's positioning on inclusivity. Marlen and RNH shared how they felt their background and experiences in relation to diversity were not aligned with their institution's actions and statements on inclusivity. It is also interesting to note that Marlen and RNH self-identified as non-white individuals. These two leaders embody diversity as they are people of colour in positions where they are in a minority (Ahmed, 2012). RNH referred to feeling like an "imposter" when he joined his institution. He felt like an imposter because he noticed, on his arrival, that he stood out due to his racial background and his age. He found himself in what Ahmed (2012) described as a "sea of whiteness."

The composition of individuals at the senior leadership level that RNH arrived at was incongruous with the institution's statements of commitment to diversity and inclusivity. Interestingly, RNH's leadership actions reveal his preference to operate in the background. An equity, diversity, and inclusion committee has been instituted at RNH's institution; however, RNH is not actively participating in it, although members of the team he leads are actively engaged in the committee. Ahmed (2012) described how sometimes people of colour working in higher education institutions where they visibly stand out as different "learn to fade in the background" (p. 42). RNH sees his leadership role as one of facilitation. He also emphasizes the importance of consultation and inclusivity in decision-making. The image of the tree with many colourful leaves that he shared highlights his leadership style in that it is the leaves that are meant to shine. The leaves represent his team and can also represent students. It would appear that RNH's conceptualization of leadership aligns with what Dei (2019) described as leadership from Indigenous and African perspectives, which is "less about individual attributes and skills than shared community expectations and roles" (p. 354) and social justice leadership practices where the voices of underrepresented and marginalized groups are heard at the discussion table.

In contrast, Marlen engages in activities that question the status quo and that call for critical self-introspection in everyone with the hope of creating a more inclusive campus community. For Marlen, the institution has verbally defined diversity and inclusivity rather than practically "embedding a culture of curiosity, embedding a culture of communal inquiry to understand what are the needs of the demographics you are serving." Her leadership practices in the communal domain suggest that she engages in self-authoring and self-transforming ways of knowing. Her leadership practices include, for example, bringing historically marginalized people to the forefront so that they can tell their own stories in their own voices. She has organized events during Black History Month, for example, that have allowed individuals from minority groups a space to participate in the main campus events and generate knowledge with other individuals.

Implicit bias. Understanding how postsecondary leaders' perceptions of diversity shape the institution's culture of inclusivity also calls for an exploration of implicit bias, also referred to in the literature as unconscious bias, in the various dimensions that leadership practices occur: personal, interpersonal, communal, and systemic. Smith et al. (2017) listed and described 12 unconscious or implicit biases in postsecondary institutions. Three of the 12 biases are of particular interest to this study: affinity bias and homosocial reproduction, resume racism and accent bias, and canonical and curriculum biases.

Affinity bias and homosocial reproduction can perhaps be described as one of the more challenging aspects of inclusivity efforts for leaders in this study. Some leaders, who have engaged in critical self-reflection, acknowledged affinity bias as a challenge they face in the personal dimension that impacts the systemic dimension, such as in the hiring and recruitment process. Orla described how she is aware of unconscious bias that leads to "insiders replicating themselves by selecting new colleagues with similar backgrounds and demographic characteristics" (Smith et al., 2012 as cited in Henry et al., 2017, p. 281). In thinking through the integrated social justice leadership framework, I realize that Orla shared how, in the personal dimension, she critically explores her ways of thinking and knowing. Because of this awareness, she attempts to monitor her assumptions when making recruitment decisions: "I always do think about that when I am recruiting. To not just gravitate to people who are like me. And by 'like me,' that might be white, that might also be style, you know." She shared that she has tried not to make assumptions about individuals with names that suggest they are from a particular country. Although she reflected on and monitored her implicit bias in the recruitment and hiring process, Orla did not share any reflections on her relative position of power. This leaves me to wonder if, as a leader, she is aware of her relative position of power and the resulting advantages and disadvantages it may bring to her as she engages in leadership practices.

Affinity bias, which leaders may or may not be aware of, is not limited to the recruitment and hiring process. Alex described a challenge that she faces as a leader with faculty members who do not see the heterogeneity in the student population and the diverse teaching and learning needs of students. She shared that some faculty treat all students as though they come from a middle-class background and expect them to follow a linear pathway to successfully obtain postsecondary credentials. Based on the conversation with Alex, and in thinking through the integrated social justice leadership framework for diversity and inclusivity, I add that such faculty members are perhaps instrumental knowers who are inclined to the "right ways of performance" (Drago-Severson & Blum-DeStefano, 2017, p. 465). Alex attributed this way of knowing to the sociohistorical backgrounds of these faculty members. According to Smith et al. (2017), "unconscious biases draw upon personal, social, and historical experiences as well as contemporary cultural references from our families and neighborhoods, from the media, and in daily life" (p. 264). Alex explained that the homogeneity in the current faculty composition has presented a limitation in terms of awareness of the needs of diverse students. She shared that the current faculty members are largely individuals who have postgraduate credentials and come from privileged backgrounds. The life experiences of these faculty members are very different from those of the students they teach. Leaders like Alex, who, according to the integrated social justice leadership framework, can be described as self-authoring and possibly self-transforming knowers, are presented with a challenge in the interpersonal domain of leading others who may not share similar ways of knowing and do not approach matter of diversity and inclusivity with the same openness.

Smith et al. (2017) discussed how resume racism, name bias, and accent bias negatively impact applicants from racialized minority populations. The scholars referenced several Canadian studies that show a tendency towards resume racism and a triple bias against racialized minorities caused by "foreign names," "foreign credentials," and "foreign experience." The implicit biases led racialized minorities, particularly those from India, China, and Pakistan, to struggle in the Canadian job market. (p. 285)

Some leaders in this study are conscious of these implicit biases and struggle with them. During the interview, Orla shared this struggle and how she constantly monitors her biases during the hiring and recruitment process:

I will tell you a struggle I do have. Seeing a resume from a person whose maybe teaching and academic experience is from a different country and maybe they do have a name that's very different from what I am used to and I am going, "Okay, this person, you know, try not to dismiss them because they don't have that Canadian teaching. They have the teaching experience. They have the academic thing. Bring them in. See how they do." Those are definitely things that I have to think about all the time when looking at resumes and not just gravitating [to people similar to me].

Affinity bias, homosocial reproduction, resume racism, and accent bias are implicit biases that affect the personal, interpersonal, communal, and systemic dimensions of social justice leadership practice. Leaders' ways of knowing play a part in the final recruitment decisions that are made. Later in this chapter I revisit recruitment challenges and discuss these in conjunction with issues of representation.

Canonical and curriculum biases refer to how "curriculum is white, Eurocentric, and colonial, and continues to reflect historical biases against women, indigenous and racialized scholars, and scholarship from non-Western countries" (Smith et al., 2017, p. 279). Leaders such as Stella, Alex, Renee, and John Thomas spoke about the Indigenization of curriculum efforts as their institutions, which, according to the integrated social justice leadership framework for diversity and inclusivity, pertain to the systemic dimension of leadership practice, social justice issue of race, and various ways of knowing. From a social justice perspective, Dei (2000) challenged educators to ask themselves: Who is teaching? "How is our curriculum diversified to ensure that we are telling multiple stories? How are we making the knowledge and education relevant to the communities from where we draw our students?" (p. 243). Lopez (2016) and Lopez and Olan (2018) challenged educators to engage with diversity from a critical perspective and engage culturally responsive and socially just practices that attend to the learning needs of students that have been historically excluded. Conversations with the leaders in this study indicate an awareness of the biases in the current curriculum. Stella shared in depth her awareness of curriculum biases during the interview. As a leader, she has sought to address these biases through her doctoral research and curriculum development work for student programs at her institution that honour Indigenous ways of being and knowing.

It is critical to note that in her role as a leader on Indigenizing the curriculum, Stella sought input from and collaboration with Indigenous groups. Based on the conversation with Stella, I would perhaps describe her as a self-transforming knower, one who "yearn[s] for interconnection and co-construction of meaning" (Drago-Severson & Blum DeStefano, 2017, p. 465) and for whom "collaboration is approached as an opportunity to mutually expand thinking" (Drago-Severson & Blum DeStefano, 2017, p. 465). Her leadership actions in curriculum development transcended the personal domain to include the interpersonal dimension where relationships with Indigenous representatives were built. In the communal dimension, Stella ensured that the Indigenous stakeholders were equal participants in the cocreation of the curriculum. In so doing, she sought to address injustices in the systemic dimension. At the time of the interview, this collaboration was working well in informing the curriculum development work and in engaging Indigenous communities.

Interestingly, John Thomas pointed out the invisibility of Indigenous people at the Western Deans of Science discussion tables on Indigenizing the science curriculum. He said that nobody at the leadership table knows how to Indigenize the science curriculum; as a result, this issue remains unaddressed. This invisibility reflects the gap in representation of Indigenous scholars and knowledge in postsecondary leadership. The missing voice of Indigenous people at this discussion table leads me to reflect on the role of representation, power, and inclusive decision-making with regard to curriculum. Shields (2002) described how power imbalances exist in curriculum decision-making. I attend to questions of representational diversity in a later chapter of this book.

Addressing canonical and curriculum biases, and affinity bias and homosocial reproduction, requires what Shields (2002) described as embracing diverse perspectives, a value needed for the development of an inclusive school community, and what Lopez and Olan (2018) described as disruptive pedagogy. The Alberta School Councils' Association (2019) has advocated for capacity building, which may be referred to as growth in the learning of education professionals so they can "develop, strengthen and renew their understanding, skills and abilities to create flexible and responsive learning environments" (Principles of Inclusive Education section, para. 5). Though this refers to K-12 education, I argue that this growth in learning is just as important in postsecondary settings when taking into consideration all the ways of knowing. Leaders in some institutions stated that they have participated in professional development opportunities that address intercultural communication skills, leadership, diversity, and inclusion matters at their institutions. Some leaders who are aware of their implicit biases, like Orla, have participated in professional development opportunities that focus on increasing their knowledge on mitigating these assumptions.

Other leaders, such as Marlen and Stella, take professional learning a step further by creating opportunities for faculty members to learn about diversity and inclusivity matters through professional development. In addition to Indigenizing the curriculum, Stella was also leading the creation of professional development offerings for faculty on antiracism and inclusive pedagogy. It appeared to me that Stella was pursuing transgressive inclusivity in the curriculum. According to DeLuca (2013), transgressive inclusivity uses diversity "as a vehicle for the generation of new knowledge and learning experiences" (p. 334). The image Stella shared of tangled histories describes her vision for diversity and inclusivity in the postsecondary context. She described how she sees the histories of individuals as tangled and of equal significance. Being able to appreciate and embrace the significance of the tangled histories allows for the generation of knowledge in a way that is inclusive. In leading the creation of teaching and learning opportunities that address racism, promote inclusivity, and honour Indigenous knowledges, Stella has engaged in social justice leadership practices that (a) challenge the status quo of the dominant culture in the various dimensions of practice and (b) promote critical awareness and questioning for all the ways of knowing as portrayed in the integrated social justice leadership framework for diversity and inclusivity.

Conclusion

Leaders draw on personal sociohistorical experiences and they navigate implicit bias as they engage, interpret, and enact values of diversity and inclusivity in their institutions. For some leaders, there is an alignment between their conceptualization of diversity and their institution's statements and actions on inclusivity. When interpreted through the integrated social justice leadership framework for diversity and inclusivity, it appears this alignment stems from their personal sociohistorical experiences with and orientation to diversity. However, not all leaders in this study experience an alignment between their conceptualization of diversity and their institution's positioning on inclusivity. For these leaders, their personal sociohistorical experiences with and orientation to diversity is in dissonance with their institution's positioning on inclusivity. Leaders navigate biases in the various dimensions of practice. Of particular interest are affinity bias and homosocial reproduction, resume racism and accent bias, and canonical and curriculum biases.

References

Ahmed, S. (2012). *On being included: Racism and diversity in institutional life*. Duke University Press.

Alberta School Councils' Association. (2019). *Principles of inclusive education*. https://www.albertaschoolcouncils.ca/education-in-alberta/alberta-education-initiatives/principles-of-inclusion

Dei, G. (2000). Towards an Anti-racism discursive framework. In G. S. Dei & A. Calliste (Eds.), *Power, knowledge and anti-racist education* (pp. 23–40). Fernwood Publishing.

DeLuca, C. (2013). Toward an interdisciplinary framework for educational inclusivity. *Canadian Journal of Education*, 36(1), 305–348.

Drago-Severson, E., & Blum-DeStefano, J. (2017). The self in social justice: A developmental lens on race, identity, and transformation. *Harvard Educational Review*, 87(4), 457–481.

Furman, G. (2012). Social justice leadership as praxis: Developing capacities through preparation programs. *Educational Administration Quarterly*, 48(2), 191–229. https://doi.org/10.1177/0013161X11427394

Henry, F., Dua, E., James, C. E., Kobayashi, A., Li, P., Ramos, H., & Smith, M. S. (Eds.). (2017). *The equity myth: Racialization and Indigeneity at Canadian universities*. University of British Columbia Press.

Kouzes, J. M., & Posner, B. Z. (2012). *The leadership challenge: How to make extraordinary things happen in organizations* (5th ed.). Jossey-Bass.

Lopez, A. E. (2016). *Culturally responsive and socially just leadership: From theory to action*. Palgrave MacMillan

Lopez, A. E., & Olan, E. L. (2018). *Transformative pedagogies for teacher education: Moving towards critical praxis in an era of change*. Information Age Publishing.

Northouse, P. (2016). *Leadership: Theory and practice*. Sage Publications.

Shields, C. M. (2002). Cross-cultural leadership and communities of difference: Thinking about leading diverse schools. In K. Leithwood (Ed.), *Second international handbook of educational leadership and administration* (pp. 209–224). Kluwer Academic Publishers.

Smith, M., Gamarro, K., & Toor, M. (2017). A dirty dozen: Unconscious race and gender biases in the academy. In F. Henry, E. Dua, C. E. James, A. Kobayashi, P. Li, H. Ramos, & M. S. Smith (Eds.), *The equity myth: Racialization and Indigeneity at Canadian Universities* (pp. 263–296). University of British Columbia Press.

· 4 ·

ENGAGING INSTITUTIONAL STRATEGIC DIRECTION AND CULTURE

Introduction

The third theme to emerge as a finding in my study and that I present in this chapter is that to make meaning of diversity and inclusivity, leaders engage their institution's strategic direction. Nine leaders shared their knowledge, perspectives and experiences with diversity and inclusivity with me through in-depth interviews, artifacts, and documents. Some leaders shared with me publicly available documents that describe their institution's strategic plan on diversity and inclusivity. These documents and the knowledge the leaders shared provided a view of how their understanding of their institution's culture of inclusivity informs their conceptualizations of diversity. The strategic direction of an institution impacts strongly on how postsecondary education leaders understand, interpret, and implement diversity and inclusivity in their leadership roles. Most leaders in this study referred to the statements of commitment to values of diversity and inclusivity listed in the strategic plan of their institution as the guide for the work they do in their respective areas. Strategic plans typically describe the institution's vision and mission statements as well as priority areas for development and growth. In this section, I consider the role of institutional culture and the strategic plan through the integrated social justice leadership framework for diversity and inclusivity.

Theme 3: Leaders Engage Their Institution's Strategic Direction on Diversity and Inclusivity

The institutional strategic plan plays an integral role in how some leaders embody diversity and inclusivity. John Thomas, Orla, and Renee have gained knowledge on diversity and inclusivity as a result of their institution's strategic direction on diversity and inclusivity. John Thomas indicated, "Until recently I was very wishy-washy about it—it didn't really matter, we are scientists, all we're focusing is on the science, deliver the science, let every student find their way to it." Orla revealed, "In fact, perhaps my sense of inclusivity has been formed by my experience working at this institution for the last 10 years." Additionally, Orla stated that through the strategic direction, she had "learned a lot and it's also shown me how much more I have to learn as well."

The Indigenization strategy at Renee's institution has resulted in the building of partnerships with Indigenous communities and in increased knowledge for Renee. She stated: "Yeah. We've established partnerships with some Indigenous communities as well. And so, through those partnerships and engaging with those great colleagues, I think too I've learned a lot and the campus has been enriched by that."

The strategic plan guides leaders such as John Thomas, Orla, Renee, and Kelli in implementing ways to reach the strategic goals for inclusivity. During the interview, Orla shared a handbill of the institution's strategic plan to show me what inspires her in it:

> The institution prides itself on, well right now our slogan for the strategic plan ... for me what resonated is this because this is relatively new. We have language around inclusivity in our vision and mission statements.... When this was being developed and being launched, and I was communicating to my own staff, actually one thing I did with them was sit with them and share with them and say here are the things that stand out to me and are kind of important to me.

The image that Orla shared with me reflected the vision and mission statements captured in the strategic plan. She drew a person with a number of stripes, with each stripe representing a dimension of diversity: "This is race, gender, socioeconomic class, life experience, religious background, family of origin, structure. Like we all have these different strands in each one of us."

At John Thomas' institution, an Equity, Diversity, and Inclusion Committee was created as a part of the strategic plan. John Thomas is a member of this committee, which has influenced how he understands inclusivity. He shared:

> In fact, up until this committee, which I actually said was only 3 or a few months ago, my understanding of inclusivity was very, too general, very broad. I knew we were doing a lot of these; we were trying to be inclusive and trying to address all learners, but it was very … I wouldn't say superficial, but it was a minor aspect of what we do, as far as I'm concerned.

As an associate dean and a member of this committee, John Thomas drew a connection between the strategic plan and the science Faculty:

> It is actually what we've declared in the strategic plan, and this is why what we are doing in science, we're not reinventing anything, we're simply trying to actually fulfil what we have declared or at least what the strategic plan has declared as one of its major goals.

The image that John Thomas shared with me during the interview reflects the goals of the institution's strategic plan. John Thomas described his image as follows:

> You have around the table, you have a number of learners and some are old, there's some are young and some are brown, some are white, or others are in between. Then you also have gender, there are males, there are females. And they're also using all different devices. Some are using keyboards, some are using tablets, some are using cell phones. What we are trying to do is, we are trying to allow our content to be accessible to learners of all forms, shapes, and sizes. We want them to be able to access our content and acquire from it exactly the maximum amount of information that we would like, using all means of delivery. You can see there, there is one of who sends an email and the other one is on wi-fi. Then there is a keyboard and then there's all sorts of delivery.

For John Thomas, this image speaks to the strategic direction that the institution is taking. His role to help ensure inclusivity, particularly through digital access. The tools and technology used to access learning materials must be accessible to all. Curriculum must be within reach for all. John Thomas stated,

> We want all learners to be able to learn what we present them, irrespective of their age, their gender, their race, their physical impairments, or whether they're blind or whether they can hear properly and even cognitive impairment. Which is, it's a big ambition.

Similarly, Kelli is dean at an institution that also has a strategic direction on diversity and inclusivity encompassing technology. Executive leadership has provided her with the support needed to actualize the strategic goals. Kelli stated that her supervisor, the vice-president academic,

> is driving what we need to do in VR [virtual reality], in AI [artificial intelligence]. I'm driving it for the people that I supervise. I'm open to it and am enjoying it. And so, as the VP pushes me to move forward in it, I'm embracing it and then helping others understand what it can look like.

One of the images Kelli provided in the collage she shared is of a computer lab representing technology in teaching and learning and the direction being taken by the institution. She declared, "That's part of our vision and mission is to shape the future of postsecondary education. And I mean a computer lab is actually passe now…. But it's really, really, we have to think about technology and being inclusive of the technology."

The institutional strategic plan plays an integral role in how leaders embody diversity and inclusivity in their institutions. It is important to note that there is an interaction between the institutional strategic plan and leaders' personal sociohistorical experiences that influence the realization of diversity and inclusivity efforts in institutions. In some instances, there is an alignment between a leader's sociohistorical experiences and the institutional strategic plan. In other instances, there is a misalignment. In this case study, the misalignment was noted by two leaders who identified as people of colour. This leads me to wonder what in their sociohistorical experiences impacts the alignment with the strategic direction on diversity and inclusivity that their institutions are pursuing. In these leaders' views, what the institutions do is not consonant with what the institutions profess about diversity and inclusion.

Interpreting Institutional Strategic Direction and Culture

So it is actually what we've declared in the strategic plan, and this is why what we are doing in science, we're not reinventing anything, we're simply trying to actually fulfil what we have declared or at least what the strategic plan has declared as one of its major goals. (John Thomas)

Ahmed (2012) argued that "institutions provide a frame in which things happen (or don't happen) ... [and] we need to ... think about words, texts, objects, and bodies, to follow them around, to explore what they do and do not do, when they are put into action" (p. 50). For several leaders in this study, regardless of their ways of knowing, the strategic plan informs their daily leadership work in the various dimensions of practice in actioning values of diversity and inclusivity. The strategic plan plays an integral role in how these leaders embody diversity and inclusivity. For John Thomas, being a member of the Equity, Diversity, and Inclusion Committee at his institution has been an illuminative experience at a personal level. The initiatives that this committee has embarked on and that John Thomas is involved in focus on diversity and inclusivity in the curriculum, which falls in the systemic dimension in the integrated social justice leadership framework. From his perspective, there is a desire to change the organizational culture of his institution to become one that is inclusive of diversity. Through this committee, John Thomas has gained increased knowledge and appreciation for inclusivity in the curriculum. He shared that prior to the formation of this committee, his understanding and appreciation of inclusivity was "too general, very broad ... a minor aspect of what we do." The establishment of the Equity, Diversity and Inclusion Committee is a step that scholars (Burke, 2013; Hughes, 2015) have said is important in cultivating a culture that is inclusive of diversity. The establishment of such a committee may be indicative of a desire to address injustices in the systemic dimension.

The institutional strategic plan appears to be a motivator for some leaders to critically reflect on "inequities and injustices that lead to the marginalization and exclusion of those who should be full participants in their organizations" (Shields, 2002, p. 219). Because of the strategic plan, John Thomas had to critically reflect on his implicit biases regarding diversity and inclusivity in the teaching and learning of sciences. Through his leadership activities, he has gained an appreciation for inclusivity of diverse learners in order to ensure that the needs of all learners are met. As leader of a science faculty, promoting successful participation of female students in the STEM disciplines has been a priority. Furthermore, he has had to transcend the personal dimension and engage in the interpersonal dimension to lead faculty members in accomplishing the inclusivity goals detailed in the strategic plan. It is in the interpersonal domain that John Thomas has experienced challenges engaging some faculty members in implementing the curriculum changes required. Similar to the leaders in Lopez's (2016) study, John Thomas described facing resistance from faculty members who did not see value in making any changes to the curriculum in order to be inclusive.

Like John Thomas, Orla shared how she refers to the strategic plan in decisions she makes as a leader and in implementing the strategic plan goals with the faculty members she leads. The leadership practices that Orla engages align with transformational leadership practices in that, when communicating with faculty members, she draws personal connections to the strategic plan and attempts to inspire them. She invites dialogue and discussion on the strategic direction in order to focus on how teaching and learning can be inclusive. What was not immediately apparent was whether Orla challenged the status quo or encouraged her team members to question their teaching practices using a critical lens. Similarly, Kelli, a dean of a large faculty, shared how she engaged in transformational leadership practices, such as model the way, inspire a shared vision, challenge the process, evolve others to act, and encourage the heart (Kouzes & Posner, 2012). Kelli described how she inspires and motivates her team in implementing the organization's strategic plan on integrating technology in teaching and learning: "I'm driving it for the people that I supervise…. And so, as the VP pushes me to move forward in it, I'm embracing it and then helping others understand what it can look like." Although Kelli shared that she models the way and inspires a shared vision of integrating technology in teaching and learning, she did not offer any considerations of diversity and inclusivity in this plan.

In describing the images that reflect what diversity and inclusivity mean to her in a postsecondary context, Kelli's reflections echo what DeLuca (2013) described as dialogical inclusivity in the interdisciplinary framework for educational inclusivity, whereby "the dominant group honours, welcomes, and celebrates the cultural complexity of individuals" (p. 332). During our conversation, Kelli shared a picture collage that depicted how she perceived diversity and inclusivity being actualized at her institution. She shared that she perceived the physical space in the institution as being designed to create an atmosphere that reflected the diverse student population through artwork, the food market, message boards, and more. The design of the physical space speaks to the vision and mission statements of the institution. From Kelli's perspective, the physical space shows that students of diverse racial backgrounds and sexual orientations are welcome at the institution.

It appears to me that Kelli's approach to matters of diversity and inclusivity might be considered superficial in that she highlighted the way in which the physical space at the institution is designed to show these students are welcome. A critical consideration is to reflect on who is doing the welcoming. It is implicit "that those who are already given a place are *the ones who are welcoming* rather than welcomed, the ones who are in the structural position of hosts" (Ahmed, 2012, p. 42). Though some leaders, like Kelli, did not refer to or acknowledge a dominant group culture existing in their institutions, other leaders like Stella, Marlen, and RNH did. In describing the image of tangled roots that she brought to the interview, Stella revealed that the current and dominant perspective is "Western European ways being, knowing, and doing." A dominant culture in the institution still exists. It is not overtly named or labelled because it is the "norm," it is in the background, it is the lens through which inclusivity has been defined in institutions and the lens through which strategic plans have been articulated. It is the dominant culture, the norm, the acknowledged resident that welcomes "others."

Stella, Marlen, and Alex, leaders who present as self-authoring and self-transforming knowers, acknowledged that there is a dominant lens through which actions in the institution are carried out. From their combined perspectives, which resonate with the literature, this lens is white, Western European, male, and able-bodied (Dei, 2000; James, 2011a; Lopez, 2016; Smith, 2017). It is not a neutral lens. The challenge is that not all leaders are aware of the lens through which they perceive the world, or the limitations that are part of that lens. Not being cognizant of this limitation leads to practices in the institution that, on the one hand, according to Ahmed (2012), appear to be inclusionary, such as celebrating multicultural events through potlucks, and on the other hand, are exclusionary in that those who do not hold the dominant lens are the "other" or are considered as guests who are to be welcomed and celebrated. Ahmed remarked that "people of color are welcomed on *condition* they return that hospitality by integrating into a common organizational culture, or by being diverse, and allowing institutions to celebrate their diversity" (p. 43). Ahmed further stated that "this very structural position of being the guest, or the stranger, the one who receives hospitality, allows an act of inclusion to maintain the form of exclusion" (2012, p. 43). One may argue that celebrating diversity is important for raising awareness and is a part of the inclusivity process. Although this argument may hold, leaders like Marlen advocate for inclusionary practices that extend beyond a celebratory nature to challenge the status quo and result in members of an institution engaging in critical self-reflection on their roles in actioning strategic plan objectives that recognize, appreciate, and engage diverse ways of knowing and generating diverse knowledge.

Ahmed (2012) stated that statements of commitment to values of diversity and inclusivity can be viewed in an institution as a pledge or as binding. John Thomas and Orla viewed the statements of commitment listed in the strategic plan as binding. As such, these leaders referenced their activities to the strategic plan. Not all leaders explicitly referred to the strategic plan during the interviews. However, their actions as leaders reflect a form of commitment to values of diversity and inclusivity. Ahmed stated that an institutional commitment to diversity can be viewed as "what an institution is behind or gets behind" (p. 114). It appears that some postsecondary institutions represented in this study get behind or support professional development opportunities that build capacity in matters of diversity and inclusion. Some institutions also get behind curriculum development and student life services that support their Indigenization strategies. Even though an institution may get behind a diversity and inclusivity commitment, some leaders face challenges that Ahmed has described as "institutional habit" and the "brick wall." Ahmed shared that "institutional habits refer not only to what an institution does or tends to do but also how certain people become habituated within institutions – how they come to occupy spaces that have already been given to them" (2012, p. 123). Ahmed also shares that a brick wall is "that which keeps its place even when an official commitment to diversity has been given" (2012, p. 174). This metaphorical brick wall appears to be more visible to those leaders with self-authoring and self-transforming ways of knowing, particularly in the systemic dimension of leadership practice. Some leaders who endeavour to actualize their institution's strategic plan commitments to diversity and inclusivity experience challenges in the personal, interpersonal, and systemic dimensions of leadership practice. In the next chapter, I take up the notions of institutional habit and brick wall and explore these through a discussion on representational diversity.

Conclusion

Institutional strategic plans play an important role in diversity and inclusivity efforts. Strategic plans guide leaders in their leadership practices in the various dimensions of praxis. The statements on diversity and inclusivity that are described in strategic plans resonate with the personal sociohistorical experiences and perspectives of some leaders. For other leaders there is dissonance. For these leaders, there is no alignment between what the institutions do and what the institutions profess about diversity and inclusivity. Questions of power and dominance are not attended to in the strategic plans shared in this study.

References

Ahmed, S. (2012). *On being included: Racism and diversity in institutional life*. Duke University Press.

Burke, L. (2013). Why we can't wait: Diversity planning in community colleges. *Community College Journal of Research and Practice, 37*(11), 839–843. https://doi.org/10.1080/106689 21003744934

Dei, G. (2000). Towards an anti-racism discursive framework. In G. S. Dei & A. Calliste (Eds.), *Power, knowledge and anti-racist education* (pp. 23–40). Fernwood Publishing.

DeLuca, C. (2013). Toward an interdisciplinary framework for educational inclusivity. *Canadian Journal of Education, 36*(1), 305–348.

Hughes, B. (2015). Recruiting, retaining, and benefiting from a diverse community college faculty: A case study of one college's successes. *Community College Journal of Research and Practice, 39*(7), 659–672. https://doi.org/10.1080/10668926.2014.885401

James, C. E. (2011a, May 15). Canada: Paradoxes of 'visible minorities' in job ads. *University World News*. https://www.universityworldnews.com/post.php?story=20110513185935314

Kouzes, J. M., & Posner, B. Z. (2012). *The leadership challenge: How to make extraordinary things happen in organizations* (5th ed.). Jossey-Bass.

Lopez, A. E. (2016). Culturally responsive and socially just leadership: From theory to action. Palgrave MacMillan

Shields, C. M. (2002). Cross-cultural leadership and communities of difference: Thinking about leading diverse schools. In K. Leithwood (Ed.), *Second international handbook of educational leadership and administration* (pp. 209–224). Kluwer Academic Publishers.

Smith, M. (2017). Disciplinary silences: Race, indigeneity, and gender in the social sciences. In F. Henry, E. Dua, C. E. James, A. Kobayashi, P. Li, H. Ramos, & M. S. Smith (Eds.), *The equity myth: Racialization and indigeneity at Canadian Universities* (pp. 239–262). University of British Columbia Press.

· 5 ·

ENCOUNTERING ISSUES OF REPRESENTATION

Introduction

Leaders encounter issues of representation in their understanding, interpretation and enactment of diversity and inclusivity in educational settings. Representational diversity refers to the visible dimensions and characteristics of diversity among people. Some leaders who shared with me their experiences, knowledge and understanding of diversity and inclusivity in postsecondary contexts disclosed that they encounter issues of representational diversity in their leadership practice. In this chapter I present the theme of representational diversity as shared with me through in-depth interviews, documents, and artifacts. I then provide an interpretation of the theme through the integrated social justice leadership framework for diversity and inclusivity in order to gain a deeper understanding of this theme in relation to diversity and inclusivity.

Theme 4. Leaders Encounter Issues of Representational Diversity

Representational diversity among leaders, especially in senior leadership positions, and in the teaching faculty favourably influences teaching and learning, student services, policies and procedures in terms of inclusivity. John Thomas and Renee described the value of representational diversity in teaching faculty as a motivator for students of different backgrounds. John Thomas explained the significance of role models for students, particularly in science, technology, engineering, and mathematics (STEM):

> I think there's nothing more persuasive than role models in any endeavour in life. You see someone who looks like you doing something, you aspire to it. You say, "I want to be like that person.… That's why in fact we have been doing what we call, our institution relations has been doing what we call women in STEM or sisters in STEM.

From the perspective of a vice-president, Renee echoed the importance of representation that John Thomas shared. She said that as her institution expanded

> there's actually a significant amount of diversity amongst the faculty and staff now. And so, I think as the staff grew, I think they just naturally brought with them a belief in diversity and inclusion. So, when a student comes, I think [they] can largely see themselves reflected amongst the staff and faculty, just really broadly in terms of ethnicity, sexual orientation.

Additionally, Renee stated, "We have a staff member who is transgender, very open, so students I think can see that and know that this is accepted and it's a safe community."

It appears that to some extent, representational diversity among senior leaders has an impact on the culture of inclusivity of the institution. Renee reported that at her institution, "there's four vice presidents, two are male, two are female. One of them is from a non-Christian faith background, the other one is an international recruit. So, there is some diversity." The diversity among the executive leaders has influenced the culture of inclusivity at the institution. For example, Renee shared that there used to be "a chapel that was on campus, a really lovely space that was really beautifully decorated. But that was reshaped to be a multifaith space…. So really intentionally tried to make that space more open, more inclusive, more diverse." Additionally, in an effort to be inclusive of Indigenous student needs, Renee shared that

> the institution hired, really excited to have an Indigenous faculty member to lead our Indigenous Studies faculty.... I think having the centre, having the manager of the centre, now having a strong faculty member who leads that work I think is also really shifting moving forward, I guess I would say, the diversity and inclusion on campus.

Although it appears that representational diversity has a positive influence on inclusivity efforts, there is a dearth of representational diversity among senior leaders. Stella and Marlen shared their observations on the lack of representational diversity among senior leadership and the resulting impact. Stella noted that her

> experience at the institution, including other postsecondary institutions, was while the learner population may be very, very diverse, possibly some of the staff and faculty getting maybe a little bit diverse [but] much less than the student population, [and] leadership is not particularly diverse. I would say that's a little different at our institution but the majority of the people sitting at the associate dean and up table are from a Western European perspective of the world.

The challenge that the lack of representational diversity presents, Stella noted, is a "perception that they [senior leaders] are neutral, their way of thinking and knowing is neutral and value free and that they are the norm and that everyone else is different." This sentiment was shared by Marlen, who pointed out that the lack of representational diversity among senior leadership could explain why institutional policies are not representative of the diversity in the student body:

> We're mid-level management, there's a bit of diversity but at the dean, director level, there's none. At the executive level, there's one out of four. It's very much a conventional[1] diversity. As a consequence, I can understand why that representation in the policies isn't there to a certain respect.

A lack of representational diversity at the senior leadership level presents a number of other challenges such as in relation to inclusivity efforts regarding curriculum. For example, efforts at John Thomas' institution to Indigenize the curriculum have not progressed much. John Thomas shared that the voice of Indigenous people is missing at the table:

There's a lot of discussions, about every dean's meeting, that meeting has brought it up and talked about doing something about it, but they have not been, and I don't know if it will give the opportunity for Indigenous people to come and speak.

Stella has been involved in Indigenizing curriculum projects at her institution. She emphasized the need to have representational diversity at high levels of leadership:

My efforts to alter that [lack of representational diversity] would be to make suggestions regarding how and who we should be approaching to be on our board of governors. How we need, at the table I sit at, to perhaps to figure out a way how to have more diverse perspectives sitting at the table because if we were to look around, we all remarkably look the same and that needs to change.

An added challenge raised by a lack of representational diversity is the impact on a leader's sense of belonging. In their careers as leaders, RNH and Alex have had experiences of not feeling they belong. RNH shared his experience in starting a senior level leadership role:

When I got here, and this is my personal experience, there's a lot of Caucasian people. I'm fortunate enough to get a role in I would call senior management, borderline executive, but it was very apparent that when I would sit around those tables that I was different. And it's not like anyone was making me feel that way, but it was very obvious that everyone looked the same and I looked different.

Not only did he look different from his colleagues, RNH further shared additional characteristics that made him feel as though he did not belong:

Age has to do with the too, because not only am I darker skinned than everyone, but I'm also younger, quite younger than the other people…. I would say there's probably two ways of looking at this. There's my perceived experiences and then actually what happens. And it's probably me in my head more than anything…. I think there's a concept that's floating around now: imposter syndrome

Alex shared how she was made to feel excluded from the educational technologies sphere because of her gender and not knowing the technical language she needed to use to get the support she needed:

I mean maybe I'm being presumptuous here, but I feel like it had to do with my age and the fact that I'm a woman. I'm not a gamer and I don't talk gaming language…. Actually the guy yesterday told me, "Bro language." He said, "You don't know bro language."

Alex felt that her agency was limited. She said, "I just took for granted some of this, my inability to have bro language, where that was putting up barriers…. You just accept it because it's been part of what we've always dealt with."

An interesting perspective shared by Marlen is that representational diversity among senior leadership has not been impactful in terms of bringing about the structural changes required for inclusivity. She shared, "I don't know that I've seen tectonic shifts, at least in postsecondary where it's, 'Look at the changes that have been made, look at the tone that has been set that is clearly representative of this person's background or identity or values.'" For leaders like Marlen, "it's been business as usual." She questioned how much influence the few senior leaders from underrepresented groups hold. From her perspective,

> There are the visible powers that be and then there are the invisible powers that be. And I think even at that point, we are leader first and then our identities after. And if you're truly committed to the role, this must come first kind of thing…. That's where I wonder if at some point people are told or they read the room.

Marlen also reflected on the demands of the leadership role and how it may be a challenge for leaders from underrepresented groups to weave their identities into their roles. She mused, "And I guess coming into leadership myself, I recognize that the expectations and the volume of work placed on you can sometimes be hard to add a piece of reflection or yourself into the work that you do."

Achieving representational diversity necessitates a consideration of hiring processes. John Thomas questioned how much effort is put into attaining representational diversity. He pointed out a discrepancy in institutions articulating statements on diversity and inclusivity and actively engaging in actions that will result in outcomes that are reflective of those values. He stated,

> I have an issue with everyone who claims to champion diversity and inclusivity, especially with the hiring business. I can tell you, in many of the positions I have sat on, and these are scores of them over the last 15 years, I would argue I have not seen any situation where faculty or at least where the committee went out of its way to be as inclusive or get visible minorities or whatever, things like that.

Marlen's image of the organizational chart summarizes the influence of representational diversity on the culture of inclusivity in postsecondary settings. For Marlen, "images of diversity at an institutional level are your org chart, and what does that look like? I think actually the images are less picturesque and more images of your policies. Images of 'What do your systems actually look like?'" Like John Thomas and Renee, Marlen shared the need for representational diversity:

> We are visual creatures. I think you need the visual of having the diversity at the top and then you need the policies to support those things because whether you're a domestic or international student, the decision falls back on the policy. If the policy reflects the realities of the students, the outcomes are going to be more favourable for them.

According to Marlen, the structural changes needed in policies requires representational diversity: "When your whole leadership demographic shifts, I think priorities can shift because you're really trying to reach the top of the top in order to really make those changes." I wonder at the possibility of achieving the leadership demographic shift that Marlen alludes in the current context where professing the value of diversity and inclusivity is not always matched with congruous action.

Interpreting Issues of Representation

While the learner population may be very, very diverse, possibly some of the staff and faculty getting maybe a little bit diverse [but] much less than the student population, [and] leadership is not particularly diverse. I would say that's a little different at our institution but the majority of the people sitting at the associate dean and up table are from a Western European perspective of the world. (Stella)

Leaders in this study highlighted the advantages of representational diversity among faculty, which is also supported in the literature (Burke, 2013; Elam & Brown, 2015; Stout et al., 2018). These advantages transcend the personal, interpersonal, communal, and systemic dimensions of social justice leadership practice. For example, John Thomas discussed the motivational impact of having female instructors or professors in the STEM fields for female students. The political discourse on increasing female representation in STEM has opened space for leaders like John Thomas to proactively engage female students in taking on STEM-related academic opportunities:

> Now for applications, for funding from the federal government for research, I remember the latest application I submitted, I was asked by our research office to specifically

state in my application that I would hire female students to work in the lab in my project because they are underrepresented in science.

Another example of the benefits of representation was described by Renee. Efforts at her institution (in response to the Truth and Reconciliation Committee's Calls to Action) in actualizing the Indigenization strategy resulted in the hiring of a Metis person as the manager of the Indigenous centre on campus and the appointment of an Indigenous faculty member to lead the Indigenous Studies faculty. These efforts have resulted in increased engagement with Indigenous students and increased knowledge of Indigenous ways of being and doing.

At the time I was working on my research project, there were national dialogues on equity and inclusion in Canadian postsecondary institutions. The focus of the dialogues in 2020, hosted by the University of Toronto, was on anti-black racism and black inclusion in higher education in Canada. During the forums, the question of representational diversity at senior leadership levels arose. What emerged during the dialogues, and is supported by research (Smith, 2019) and is also a finding in this study, is the lack of representational diversity at senior and executive leadership levels. This is reflected in Stella's observation that "overwhelmingly at the associate dean level and manager level we are talking about Caucasian people with Western European perspectives." Similarly, Marlen shared that there was some diversity among middle management but hardly any among senior management. Smith (2019) argued that despite over 33 years of initiatives in equity and diversity in Canada, the diversity gap still exists.

The current state of lack of representational diversity in leadership calls for an exploration of how leaders occupy space as it relates to diversity and inclusivity. RNH shared his experience of arriving at his institution and feeling like an "imposter." He shared that it "was very apparent that when I would sit around those tables that I was different. And it's not like anyone was making me feel that way, but it was very obvious that everyone looked the same and I looked different." He was, as Ahmed (2012) put it, "hyper visible." The "norm," the "habit," or the space that was already occupied at RNH's institution was filled by older white male leaders. RNH described how he had to remind himself that he now occupied a part of this leadership space because he had the skills and qualifications required for the position and that his colleagues respected this.

Representational diversity in leadership influences the institution's culture of inclusivity and leaders' sense of belonging. Occupying space that is not ordinarily occupied by people of colour had a bearing upon RNH's sense of belonging. In describing the image that he shared of the tree with multicoloured leaves and how this image reflects what diversity and inclusivity mean to him in a postsecondary context, RNH shared that he saw himself as a branch that is "in the background playing the role that I play in terms of all the things I described around structure and integrity." I observed with interest that RNH prefers to recede from his hypervisible space and work in the background. This made me realize that what Ahmed (2012) noted as the propensity for minority leaders to legitimize their existence, which can lead them to choose to reduce their visibility as RNH did.

Reducing one's visibility as a minority leader seems to be a double-edged sword. A leader like RNH, who occupies a leadership space which is not ordinarily occupied by persons of color cannot help but be visible. Such a leader may be expected by other leaders in the institution to champion diversity and inclusivity initiatives that satisfy these other leaders' expectations of what needs to be accomplished. I emphasize *other leaders' expectations* given that there is no agreed-upon conceptualization of diversity (Janssens & Steyaert, 2003). Furthermore, other leaders' expectations are perhaps informed by their ways of knowing. In my experience as a female leader of colour who is hypervisible, I have observed that engaging with individuals who can be defined as instrumental knowers, who "have a concrete, right/wrong orientation to their work and the world and have not yet developed the internal capacity to more fully take another's perspective" (Drago-Severson & Blum DeStefano, 2017, p. 464), places an immense amount of pressure on leaders from underrepresented populations. Instrumental knowers are not able to see the realities of marginalized populations or the role they play in the existing social structures that give privilege to some and not to others. When working with instrumental knowers, the "burden" of casting a social justice lens on teaching and learning matters and of advocating for social justice concerns to be addressed falls on leaders from underrepresented populations. Such work is emotionally and mentally exhausting for leaders like RNH. It is, therefore, not surprising that some leaders may prefer to work in the background.

In discussing with Marlen the issue of representational diversity, identity, and racialized senior leaders at her institution, she expressed some frustration with what she perceived as ineffective impact in forwarding the diversity and inclusivity agenda: "But I feel like I don't know that I've seen tectonic shifts."

She wondered "if at some point [racialized] people are told [they can't make these shifts] or they read the room." Leaders who are hypervisible in the room may feel they do not belong there and are psychologically legitimizing their presence while carrying out the tasks their positions require. In reading the room, leaders like RNH know that there is already a misalignment between their personal sociohistorical experiences and the institution's positioning on diversity and inclusivity. A leader in this position could decide to recede from hypervisibility and consequently be deemed ineffective by peers in bringing about dramatic change. Alternatively, this leader, particularly if they are a self-transforming knower, could decide to increase their hypervisibility by exposing the misalignment they experience and pushing forward an agenda that may not be what the "institution gets behind." There are risks associated with increased hypervisibility.

Racialized leaders who increase their already hypervisible status may run the risk of being perceived as "the angry person of color" (Ahmed, 2012, p. 143). Marlen, similar to RNH, is hypervisible in the leadership room. Also, like RNH, for Marlen there is not an alignment between her personal socio-historical experiences and her institution's stated position on inclusivity. Unlike RNH, however, Marlen does not recede to the background. The leadership practices she has engaged were motivated by what she felt needed to be done: "And I was putting things out there based off of what I was seeing in social media, current events, my own kind of pieces of advocacy." Some of these practices included facilitating learning opportunities in the form of workshops where she challenged participants to question themselves and reflect on the following questions: "Am I supporting a system? Am I embodying a system? What is the system that I'm so comfortable with?" In relation to the integrated social justice leadership framework for diversity and inclusivity, Marlen challenged the workshop participants to engage their ways of knowing and ask critical questions related to diversity and inclusivity that impact the personal and systemic dimensions of practice. The feedback that she received after facilitating one such workshop was that participants felt she was calling them all racist. This was not the intended outcome of the workshop. Her intention was for the participants to gain awareness of the spaces they inhabit and how those spaces are not inclusive of diversity in the various dimensions of social justice practice. The workshop participants, however, understood this differently. In reflecting on Marlen's leadership experiences with diversity and inclusivity, I realize that she perhaps was coming up against the brick wall, that which keeps its place, as described by Ahmed (2012). The daily institutional practices, who occupies leadership spaces in the institution, what values, beliefs, and language are made visible and honoured can be a brick wall for leaders like Marlen and RNH.

Navigating the metaphorical brick wall is a challenge that leaders experience differently. For Stella, a challenge she experiences with members of senior leadership is the perspective that "they are neutral, their way of thinking and knowing is neutral and value free and that they are the norm and that everyone else is the different." This perspective presents a challenge in creating an organizational culture that extends beyond the cursory welcoming and celebrating of diverse groups of people. In describing her artifact of the tree trunk and tangled roots, Stella described a world where diversity and inclusion mean that the various perspectives and world views serve to generate new knowledge (DeLuca, 2013) that "critically examine[s] the socially constructed ways of making meaning in a racialized, gendered, and classed world" (Dei, 2000, p. 25). Indigenizing the curriculum in the academic programs that she oversees is an experience she shared where Indigenous worldviews and perspectives were not simply welcomed and celebrated but had space in the cocreation of the curriculum. Various Indigenous stakeholders were represented.

The lack of representational diversity at senior leadership is problematic for inclusivity in curriculum development. John Thomas described the challenges that his and other institutions experience with Indigenizing science curricula. Interestingly, he noted that there has not been any Indigenous representation at the discussion table. John Thomas provided an example of how in science, for instance, one would use Newton's laws of physics to explain an apple falling from a tree. This example is drawn from a Western European perspective and understanding of physics. Goodman and Bond (1993, as cited in Loreman, 2007) stated that the curricula of a number of Western countries tend "to be linear, inflexible, divorced from context, overly specific, centralized, and unresponsive to the needs of minority groups" (p. 28). The brick wall to inclusivity that leaders like John Thomas face with Indigenizing the science curriculum lies in the institutional habits—the norm from which the curriculum is designed, and the perspectives of those who teach science curriculum and those who make decisions regarding the curriculum in the systemic dimension. Indigenous voices are not at the leadership table where decisions are made. Research by Smith (2019) showed that "Indigenous women and men are largely notable for their near absence" (p. 4) in senior and executive leadership.

The increase in international students on postsecondary campuses in Alberta has led to increased racial diversity. Teaching faculty members are faced with increased numbers of international students in their classrooms, and there is an expectation that educational outcomes and teaching practices prepare all students to live and work in a much more intercultural and global economy. Orla, Alex, and Marlen discussed some of the conflicts that arise between teaching faculty and international students, particularly with regard to academic integrity. Orla and Alex described how, as leaders, they constantly monitor their assumptions about international students when navigating issues relating to academic integrity. During the interview, Marlen spoke of the need to address who is teaching and what teaching methods are being used to meet the learning needs of international students. This brings me back to the integrated social justice leadership framework for diversity and inclusivity, whereby an individual's approach to diversity and inclusivity in the personal dimension influences their practices in the other dimensions. In order to challenge the existing system and curriculum, and to ask critical questions of representation, leaders need to approach social justice issues from a self-transforming position, a position that acknowledges that their identities and systems are limited and form only a perspective of the whole. The changing demographics on postsecondary campuses call for leaders to consider representation in faculty members, in the curriculum, and in the ways of generating knowledge.

In discussing representational diversity with some of the participants, issues relating to hiring and recruitment practices were raised. Diversity is a part of the hiring discourse in that diversity and inclusion statements are placed on recruitment calls. Though the wording on the recruitment calls varies by institution, the messaging usually includes an invitation to individuals from underrepresented and minority populations to apply and states that the institution is committed to values of diversity and inclusivity. Despite the diversity and inclusivity statements on recruitment materials, some leaders in this study raised the point that there seemed to be very little attention given to inclusive hiring practices. Alex shared, "I think this is one area where the institution maybe could do better is that we often are hiring people that are the same." The homogeneity in faculty members presents a challenge for a leader like Alex in that faculty cannot identify with the life experiences and challenges students face. Furthermore, the perspectives or worldviews that a homogenous faculty brings are not inclusive of the needs of diverse students. Alex illustrated this point with the bookshelf image she discussed in the interview, whereby there is a desire by some faculty members to have all the books on the shelf organized in a particular order. In thinking through the integrated social justice leadership framework for diversity and inclusivity, Alex faces the challenge of the metaphorical brick wall in the interpersonal and systemic dimensions with faculty members who perhaps approach diversity from ways of knowing that differ from hers. One of the benefits of diversity in faculty that is missed when representational diversity is lacking is that the greater the diversity among faculty, the higher the graduation rates for under-represented minority students (Stout et al., 2018). The benefits of diversity in faculty are well documented. Despite the evidence, representational diversity is still lacking. There is a need to better understand the hiring and recruitment experiences of leaders that result in reproducing a homogenous faculty and leadership.

An additional challenge to the issue of representational diversity in the hiring process was described by John Thomas: "I have not seen any situation where faculty or at least where the [hiring] committee went out of its way to be as inclusive or get visible minorities." He went on further to state "we are not going to hire someone who is underqualified simply because they are a minority." Orla shared similar struggles. James and Chapman-Nyaho (2017) stated that "the notion of qualification is placed in opposition to diversity, in that to take into account the race of candidates was thought to mean hiring someone who was 'less qualified.'" (p. 102). One often hears how the person who is "best qualified" or the "best fit" for the position gets hired. It is interesting to note that the beliefs and values that influence the hiring practices result in the majority of those who are hired and who occupy leadership spaces forming a homogenous group, thus keeping in place the "norm" or the "habit." James (2017) called for the discourse on diversity to include a challenging of the role of power and dominant beliefs in order to stop reinforcing stereotypes regarding the competencies and skills of racialized minority applicants that render them not "the best fit."

Furthermore, some leaders in this inquiry identified that one of the challenges in the hiring process is that the pool of candidates to select from is limited. John Thomas shared an example of this: "We had a position recently in, well I think in architecture, and we had about 12 to 13 applications. The majority of them, about, for some reason, five or six of those 13, were from one country." John Thomas speculated that the reason for such a high number of applicants from one country could be "because that country has a very good architecture school or culture in architecture, and so they have been training lots of architects all the time and they are very keen in architecture." Though this reason could be a contributing factor, it is worth considering the ecological dimension of the integrated social justice leadership framework for diversity and inclusivity and the role the political discourse on immigration plays as possible contributing factors.

According to the *Annual Report to Parliament on Immigration* (Immigration, Refugees and Citizenship Canada, 2018), in 2017 the Government of Canada granted permanent residency status to individuals from over 185 countries. The top three countries where permanent residents came from were India, the Philippines, and China, respectively. India and the Philippines were among the top three source countries in 2016 as well. It is not surprising, therefore, that a candidate pool may have a disproportionate number of Canadian immigrant applicants from one region of the world. The example shared by John Thomas and research documented by Henry et al. (2017) indicate that racialized individuals apply for faculty positions; however, research also shows that postsecondary teaching faculty and leadership lack representational diversity (Jeffcoat & Piland, 2012; Smith, 2017). The leaders in this inquiry shared their personal struggles with implicit biases (affinity bias, homosocial reproduction, resume racism, accent bias) during the hiring process. They also shared the challenges that they face in the interpersonal dimension with colleagues who consider themselves to be neutral in their worldview, which currently is the dominant Western European, white, and male worldview. These colleagues approach hiring of new faculty from this dominant perspective.

Scholars Kitossa et al. (2020) spoke to the need for a critical mass of representational diversity, especially at the leadership table where decisions are made. Smith (2017) took up critical mass to mean a state "in which women and racialized minorities constitute a cohort large enough that it disrupts notions of tokenism and the experiences associated with the politics of being alone" (p. 245). Achieving representational diversity in postsecondary leadership that is reflective of the student demographic and the broader community could perhaps allow for a critical mass that would alleviate hypervisibility and the sense of not belonging, and the burden of representing and speaking for a racialized or minority group.

Conclusion

Representational diversity in leadership is beneficial in a number of ways particularly for learning outcomes. It also influences the culture of inclusivity in the institution. Despite the benefits documented in research, there is a dearth of representational diversity in senior leadership in postsecondary institutions. The lack of representational diversity presents a number of challenges in institutions related to curriculum and canonical biases, recruitment and hiring, and a sense of belonging and agency for racialized leaders. The lack of representational diversity in senior leadership means that structural inequities in educational settings remain intact and are not disrupted. Engaging the integrated social justice leadership framework for diversity and inclusivity in relation to representational diversity calls for critical self-reflection in all dimensions of praxis.

Note

1   "Conventional diversity" is in reference to what is typical of the status quo. Representation at the executive level is not reflective of the student population.

References

Ahmed, S. (2012). *On being included: Racism and diversity in institutional life.* Duke University Press.

Burke, L. (2013). Why we can't wait: Diversity planning in community colleges. *Community College Journal of Research and Practice, 37*(11), 839–843. https://doi.org/10.1080/106689 21003744934

Dei, G. (2000). Towards an anti-racism discursive framework. In G. S. Dei & A. Calliste (Eds.), *Power, knowledge and anti-racist education* (pp. 23–40). Fernwood Publishing.

DeLuca, C. (2013). Toward an interdisciplinary framework for educational inclusivity. *Canadian Journal of Education, 36*(1), 305–348.

Drago-Severson, E., & Blum-DeStefano, J. (2017). The self in social justice: A developmental lens on race, identity, and transformation. Harvard Educational Review, 87(4), 457–481.

Elam, C., & Brown, G. (2005). The inclusive university: Helping minority students choose a college and identify institutions that value diversity. *Journal of College Admission, 187,* 14–17.

Henry, F., Dua, E., James, C. E., Kobayashi, A., Li, P., Ramos, H., & Smith, M. S. (Eds.). (2017). *The equity myth: Racialization and indigeneity at Canadian universities.* University of British Columbia Press.

Immigration, Refugees and Citizenship Canada. (2018). *Annual report to Parliament on immigration.* https://www.canada.ca/content/dam/ircc/migration/ircc/english/pdf/pub/annual-rep ort-2018.pdf

James, C. E. (2017). "You know why you were hired, don't you?": Expectations and challenges in university appointments. In F. Henry, E. Dua, C. E. James, A. Kobayashi, P. Li, H. Ramos, & M. S. Smith (Eds.), *The equity myth: Racialization and indigeneity at Canadian Universities* (pp. 155–170). University of British Columbia Press.

James, C. E., & Chapman-Nyaho, S. (2017). "Would never be hired these days": The precarious work situation of racialized and Indigenous faculty members. In F. Henry, E. Dua, C. E. James, A. Kobayashi, P. Li, H. Ramos, & M. S. Smith (Eds.), *The equity myth: Racialization and indigeneity at Canadian Universities* (pp. 84–114). University of British Columbia Press.

Janssens, M., & Steyaert, C. (2003). Theories of diversity within organisation studies: Debates and future trajectories. *SSRN Electronic Journal.* https://doi.org/10.2139/ssrn.389044

Jeffcoat, K., & Piland, W. E. (2012). Anatomy of a community college faculty diversity program. *Community College Journal of Research and Practice, 36*(6), 397–410. https://doi.org/ 10.1080/10668920902813477

Kitossa, T., Blackfoot, A., Costen, W., Campbell, K., & Smith, M. (2020, October 2). Inclusive decision making structures [Panel discussion]. National Dialogues and Action for Inclusive Higher Education and Communities, University of Toronto, Canada.

Loreman, T. (2007). Seven pillars of support for inclusive education: Moving from "Why?" to "How? *International Journal of Whole Schooling, 3*(2), 22–38.

Smith, M. (2019). *The diversity gap in 2019: Canadian U15 universities – Leadership pipeline.* Academic Women's Association, University of Alberta. https://uofaawa.files.wordpress. com/2019/06/2019_u15_leadership_diversity_gap_release_20jun2019_final-1.pdf

Stout, R., Archie, C., Cross, D., & Carman, C. (2018). The relationship between faculty diversity and graduation rates in higher education. *Intercultural Education, 29*(3), 399–417.

· 6 ·

SITUATING DIVERSITY AND INCLUSIVITY IN THE PROVINCIAL SOCIOPOLITICAL CONTEXT

Introduction

Leaders in this study reflected on diversity and inclusivity within the provincial sociopolitical context in which they live and work in Alberta, Canada. All the nine leaders that I spoke with were leaders of postsecondary institutions in Alberta. They had all been in their leadership position for at least a year at the time of the interviews. In this chapter I share how leaders situate diversity and inclusivity in the provincial sociopolitical context as shared with me during the interviews and through documents and artifacts. The Alberta provincial election had recently taken place when I met with most of the participants. Several leaders expressed shock at the election results that brought into power the United Conservative Party (UCP). Prior to the election, the New Democratic Party (NDP) had been in power. I then interpret what was shared with me through the integrated social justice leadership framework for diversity and inclusivity to allow for a deeper understanding of this theme in relation to diversity, inclusivity, and leadership praxis.

Theme 5. Leaders Situate Diversity and Inclusivity Issues in the Provincial Sociopolitical Context

Leaders of some postsecondary institutions in Alberta have made public commitments to values of diversity and inclusivity; however, from the perspective of the participants, the provincial sociopolitical environment in which they operate is not aligned with these values. A few leaders noted how the culture outside of the postsecondary context does not embrace diversity and inclusivity. Alex drew a comparison between Alberta and three other Canadian provinces in terms of inclusivity and Indigenous populations. She noted,

> In Alberta, we have reservations [reserves] for Indigenous people, but in BC and the Yukon, Ontario, it's not set up that way. People are living and working and educating together, within a community. And so, some of the things that I see in Alberta are not things that I've seen in other provinces.

Marlen shared an experience outside of her institution that impressed upon her the hostility toward some minority groups:

> I've had a few experiences in the last year outside of postsecondary where I'm test driving a car and this guy is talking about, "Oh yeah. You know it's so frustrating to keep getting these Muslim guys and they keep haggling and they are so cheap and whatever." While I don't necessarily identify, I'm not a practicing Muslim anymore, I have a heritage and family and a dad who identify with that. And I'm just sitting in the car like, "Have you not read the room right now?"

Michelle noted the different view of her husband's colleagues with regard to diversity and inclusivity, saying, "It's interesting because my husband is in business and so every once in a while we'll get together with his business colleagues, and it's like, oh wow, they see things very differently." Michelle expressed shock and alluded to the surprise that her colleagues shared when the election results were announced: "I know when the election happened, the Alberta election, and then it was a landslide everybody here was like 'What'!" Michelle's concern at the election results centered on the rights of marginalized groups. Rhetorically she questioned,

> Do people not care about these things? Yeah, right, they don't! A lot of people don't. Like somebody asked, 'Do people out there not care about LGBTQ rights?' And it's like, I think they don't. A lot of people don't care or they like to not care about it.

Stella expressed a similar response, noting that the election results were indicative of steering away from the direction of diversity and inclusivity; however, she remained hopeful:

> With my family members and others, I see movement in what I consider to be the right direction starting slowly, not nearly as fast as I would like it to happen and certainly not in the States and not really in Alberta right now with the recent election. That's what it is! It's crazy. But I have hope.

Relating the provincial election result to the postsecondary context, Marlen shared,

> The ironic thing though is that we have a government, a provincial government, that is very much not aligned. The impression it gives is that it's inclined to be supportive of more diversity. The very tenets of their platforms is the antithesis of that. And yet they have taken money away from postsecondary and expect that we are supplementing that with international students. And the irony there is, so now you've created a social political environment that is not welcoming to anyone coming here but you are expecting them to generate money.

Some leaders felt postsecondary institutions are a "microcosm" (Michelle) or a "bubble" (Kelli) within Alberta. In her role as a dean, Kelli stated,

> In my scope, I think that it's [postsecondary is] one of the places that you will see the most diversity and inclusivity. So, when I go to any function for postsecondary, it's a lovely conversation. Rarely, if ever, do you have to experience things that are not positive around diversity and inclusivity.

In sharing her perspectives on how the postsecondary workplace context differs from other workplaces with regard to negative attitudes toward diversity and inclusivity, Kelli shared that "in postsecondary, I just haven't experienced those things that I have as I grew up or as I'm in different groups of people."

During the interviews, it became clear that some leaders believe that postsecondary institutions have a key role to play in leading the province in becoming more inclusive of diversity. Kelli said postsecondary institutions have to take the lead in the province on matters of diversity and inclusivity: "This [diversity and inclusivity] has to be broader. This has to be shared. We need to be the exemplar that moves along the population." Opportunities for being the exemplar arise through interactions with external stakeholders, such as work integrated learning partners. Kelli noted that "workplace partners make assumptions that all of our learners are international learners because of English language learning and/or other reasons that they think that they're international learners. No. We need to change that. To have different conversations." She added,

> I think that's an important role that we play as a postsecondary with work inte-
> grated learning. We have that opportunity to exchange on a constant and regular
> basis and to speak about people differently and to help others understand and not
> make assumptions.

Marlen cautioned that with taking the lead, postsecondary institutions "have to acknowledge the fact that when it comes to history, postsecondaries and those that are educated have always been attacked because they have always been the liberal-minded and they've always been the ones to uphold [inclusive values]."

Some leaders in this study have remarked on the misalignment in diversity and inclusivity values between postsecondary institutions, the provincial government, and sections of Albertan society. In order to move the Albertan population toward inclusivity, some leaders in the study advocated that postsecondary institutions lead the way and be models. A question that came to my mind is, to what extent are postsecondary institutions exemplars of diversity and inclusivity? I also wondered how leaders of postsecondary institutions can help Albertans "read the room" on matters of diversity and inclusivity.

Interpreting Situating Diversity and Inclusivity in the Provincial Sociopolitical Context

> We have a government, a provincial government that is very much not aligned. The
> impression it gives is that it's inclined to be supportive of more diversity. The very
> tenets of their platforms is the antithesis of that. (Marlen)

Leaders in this study make meaning of the phenomenon, diversity and inclusivity, by way of situating it in the Albertan sociopolitical context. In thinking through the integrated social justice leadership framework for diversity and inclusivity, it appears that some leaders in this inquiry, regardless of their ways of knowing, recognize that the social justice issues they engage at their institutions "are situated within broader sociopolitical, economic, and environmental contexts" (Furman, 2012, p. 211). This broader context is the ecological dimension of social justice leadership practice. These leaders perceived a misalignment between the provincial political issues in the community on diversity and inclusivity and their institutions' commitments to diversity and inclusivity. The fact that the misalignment is so clearly visible is a call for an exploration of the sociopolitical issues related to diversity and inclusivity in Alberta at the time this study was conducted.

In this section, I discuss these sociopolitical issues as presented by two political parties, the UCP and NDP. Participants in this study referred to the provincial election that had taken place a few months before the interviews. At the time that the interviews took place, the UCP provincial government had recently come into power, taking over from the NDP. Some leaders in this study expressed shock and concern over the sociopolitical issues discussed by the United Conservative government in relation to diversity and inclusivity. Some of the terminology that leaders in the study mentioned when sharing their thoughts on the political discourse in Alberta that I think reflect the discourse on diversity and social difference markers were "LGBTQ rights," "immigrants," "international students," "Indigenous," and "English language learners." In this section, I review, in relation to diversity and inclusivity, the 2019 election platforms of the NDP (Notley, 2019) and the UCP as well as the accomplishments listed by the United Conservative government within its first 100 days in office (United Conservatives, 2019). This provides a context in which to think through the integrated social justice leadership framework on diversity and inclusivity in relation to the views shared by leaders in this study when the shift from the NDP government to the UCP government occurred.

In discussing the sociopolitical climate in Alberta after the elections, Michelle shared: "Somebody asked, 'Do people out there not care about LGBTQ rights?' And I think they don't. A lot of people don't care or they like to not care about it." An electronic search of the keyword "LGBTQ" in the 2019 election platform documents of both parties turned up six results in the NDP platform and no results in the UCP platform. The NDP 2019 election platform document contained a section entitled "Protecting LGBTQ Albertans." In this section is information on the actions the NDP government undertook such as passing an act supporting K-12 students' rights to create or join a gay-straight alliance at school. With this act, school administrators were prevented from informing parents when students joined gay-straight alliances. This was to help ensure the safety of LGBTQ students. Within the first 100 days of coming into power, the United Conservative government introduced

Bill 8, which refuted and replaced the act passed by the previous NDP government on gay-straight alliances in educational contexts. Bill 8 made changes that some critics argue negatively impact LGBTQ students. Wells (2019) stated that with this new bill, LGBTQ students would no longer feel safe as they could be outed and the implementation of gay-straight alliances would be limited. The United Conservative government offered a divergent view, outlining how the government supports gay-straight alliances as well as an advisory on disclosing student participation in gay-straight alliances.

Marlen, whom I would describe as a self-transforming knower, pinpointed where the dissonance lies for her between the political discourse in Alberta and values of diversity and inclusivity:

> And yet they have taken money away from postsecondary and expect that we are supplementing that with international students. And the irony there is, so now you've created a social political environment that is not welcoming to anyone coming here but you are expecting them to generate money.

The 2019 budget for postsecondary institutions in Alberta was announced a couple of months before the interviews with leaders began. Overall, postsecondary institutions faced reduced provincial funding. The tuition freeze for postsecondary institutions that had been put in place by the previous NDP government was lifted. From a social justice perspective, the challenge with decreased government funding of postsecondary education and increased tuition fees is that racial minority and working-class members of the community experience barriers to accessing education (Dei, 2014). The current political discourse in Alberta focuses on international students as a revenue stream for postsecondary institutions. This discourse appears to align with the task-related knowledge, skills, and capacities categorization of diversity (McGrath et al., 1995, as cited in Janssens & Steyaert, 2003), which Janssens and Steyaert (2003) stated is an organizational and economical perspective on diversity and inclusivity. Interestingly, social justice and critical race scholar Dei (2014) warned that "we must be mindful of business-minded approaches to education, driven by profits more than by concerns of social responsibility" (p. 242).

An electronic search of the keyword "immigrant" in the 2019 NDP election platform document turned up results in a section entitled "An Inclusive and Diverse Alberta." In this section was a list of what the NDP government claimed to have achieved in creating an environment that is inclusive of diversity. For immigrants, the NDP government claimed that it made improvements to the Alberta Immigrant Nominee Program by reducing wait times and creating a fairer application to permanent residency process. Grants to support immigrant business owners and settlement services were introduced. Additionally, the NDP proposed that, if elected, they would eliminate tuition for high school upgrading and English language learning programs for adult learners as a way of removing barriers to accessing education.

In this same section of the NDP 2019 platform on an Inclusive and Diverse Alberta, was a statement on the development of an antiracism strategy and the creation of an antiracism advisory council. Additionally, the NDP government had begun a K-12 curriculum review with the goal of "ensuring Alberta students learn about racism and about the modern, diverse makeup of the province" (Notley, 2019, p. 27). Social justice and critical race scholars (Lopez, 2016; James, 2011c; Smith, 2017) have called for educational leaders to ask critical questions, such as the following: "How is our curriculum diversified to ensure that we are telling multiple stories? How are we making the knowledge and education relevant to the communities from where we draw our students?" (Dei, 2014, p. 243).

The word "racism" did not feature in the UCP platform document. The curriculum review work initiated by the NDP government was put on hold during the first 100 days of the UCP government in power. According to the UCP 2019 platform, "the social studies curriculum should be taught without political bias, offering an objective understanding of Albertan, Canadian, and world history, geography, and civic literacy" (United Conservatives, 2019, p. 58). Herein lie the epistemological and ontological differences: The position of the UCP government is that curriculum can be taught from a position of objectivity and neutrality. As argued earlier in this chapter, such a position results in the "norm," the "metaphorical brick wall," the dominant Western European perspective staying in place. Stella, who could be described as a self-transforming knower, shared the challenges that she has experienced with this hegemonic perspective in various leadership practice domains. Engaging a social justice and critical perspective in education "raises our understanding of how and why the dominant perspective shapes, for example, political opinions, religious beliefs, gender roles, and racial self-image" (Kowalchuk, 2019, Theoretical Framework section, para. 1)

Although it appears that there is a misalignment between the current political discourse on the phenomenon and institutional diversity and inclusivity statements, I argue that perhaps there is not such a misalignment. The organizational structures and culture of postsecondary institutions in Alberta reflect the provincial sociopolitical context to a large extent. Despite institutional commitments to values of diversity and inclusivity, the metaphorical "brick wall" still exists for marginalized individuals in postsecondary institutions, including leaders from historically marginalized communities. Fundamental structural issues of power relations in the various dimensions of praxis in educational settings are not addressed. Some leaders in this study pointed out that the organizational structure in postsecondary institutions needs to reflect the student demographic in order for structural changes to take place. Other leaders pointed to the need to include Indigenous ways of knowing in all the dimensions of leadership praxis in postsecondary institutions. There is misalignment for individual leaders such as Marlen, Stella, and RNH, but not at the collective institutional level. At an organizational level, the leadership lens and the leadership approach are those of the dominant Western European organizational culture. In the following section, I describe briefly an observation I made with regard to the silence on non-Western and nonheteronormative approaches to leadership in this study that is also reflected in the current sociopolitical provincial context.

Conclusion

Leaders in this study situated diversity and inclusivity in the provincial sociopolitical context in which they live and work. They expressed concern with the misalignment between the provincial sociopolitical context engagement with diversity and inclusivity with the positioning of their institutions on these values. When this theme is interpreted through the integrated social justice leadership framework for diversity and inclusivity, it becomes apparent that the institutional structures and culture of postsecondary institutions in Alberta are reflective of the provincial sociopolitical context. The fundamental structural issues of power relations, white Eurocentric ways of knowing, colonial knowledge systems are not addressed at the institutional level nor are they attended to at provincial sociopolitical level.

References

Dei, G. J. (2014). Personal reflections on anti-racism education for a global context. *Encounters on Education*, 15, 239–249.

Furman, G. (2012). Social justice leadership as praxis: Developing capacities through preparation programs. *Educational Administration Quarterly*, 48(2), 191–229. https://doi.org/10.1177/0013161X11427394

James, C. E. (2011c). Multicultural education in a color-blind society. In C.A. Grant & A. Portera (Eds.), *Intercultural and multicultural education: Enhancing global interconnectedness* (pp. 191–210). Taylor and Francis. https://doi.org/10.4324/9780203848586

Janssens, M., & Steyaert, C. (2003). Theories of diversity within organisation studies: Debates and future trajectories. *SSRN Electronic Journal*. https://doi.org/10.2139/ssrn.389044

Kowalchuk, D. (2019). Voices for change: Social justice leadership practices. *Journal of Educational Leadership and Policy Studies*, 3(1). https://files.eric.ed.gov/fulltext/EJ1226940.pdf

Lopez, A. E. (2016). *Culturally responsive and socially just leadership: From theory to action.* Palgrave MacMillan

Notley, R. (2019). *Fighting for you: Our Alberta NDP 2019 election platform.* https://rachelnotley.ca

Smith, M. (2017). Disciplinary silences: Race, indigeneity, and gender in the social sciences. In F. Henry, E. Dua, C. E. James, A. Kobayashi, P. Li, H. Ramos, & M. S. Smith (Eds.), *The equity myth: Racialization and indigeneity at Canadian Universities* (pp. 239–262). University of British Columbia Press.

United Conservatives. (2019). Alberta strong and free: Getting Alberta back to work. https://albertastrongandfree.ca/wp-content/uploads/2019/04/Alberta-Strong-and-Free-Platform-1.pdf

Wells, K. (2019, June 27). Opinion: Bill 8 will make schools less safe for all students. *Edmonton Journal*. https://edmontonjournal.com/opinion/columnists/opinion-bill-8-will-make-schools-less-safe-for-all-students

DISCURSIVE LIMITATIONS OF DIVERSITY AND INCLUSIVITY

Introduction

My conversations with nine postsecondary leaders revealed that to understand, interpret, and enact values of diversity and inclusivity in educational contexts calls for leaders draw on their personal sociohistorical experiences, navigate implicit bias, engage their institution's strategic direction on diversity and inclusivity, encounter issues of representational diversity, and they situate diversity and inclusivity in the provincial sociopolitical context. Interpreting these themes through the integrated social justice leadership framework for diversity and inclusivity shows that there are limitations with the current discourse on diversity and inclusivity. In this chapter, I begin with a discussion of the discursive limitations with the current discourse. I then extend the discussion with a view to equity and decolonial thought in educational contexts.

Discursive Limitations of Diversity and Inclusivity

Leaders in this study were largely silent on critical approaches to leadership in postsecondary contexts such as issues of historical assumptions of white

Eurocentric systems of knowledge, decolonization, colonial ways of knowing and questions of racism. Only one participant, RNH, alluded to the difference in his approach to leadership compared to his colleagues and how his cultural upbringing contributed to his leadership approach. With the exception of Stella, none of the leaders in this study spoke about Indigenous ways of leadership or nonheteronormative approaches to leadership. From the lens of the integrated social justice leadership framework, this silence confirms that current leadership theory and practice in Alberta is assumed from the dominant white Western lens (Lopez, 2021). In thinking through this silence I reflected on what Ahmed (2012) described as the comfortable nature of the current discourse on diversity and inclusivity.

While some leaders have used the current discourse on diversity to further efforts on inclusivity in their institutions, social justice issues of colonial knowledge systems, white Eurocentric ways of knowing, and racism remain intact. The language of diversity and inclusivity has come to refer to those who look different (Ahmed, 2012) and it has simply become a code word for race (James, 2011b). In addition, it has removed the sense of urgency and accountability that is evoked when words such as injustice, inequity, or decolonization (Lopez, 2021; Ahmed, 2012) are used to discuss historical forms of oppression and questions of racism and in the colonial context of education. It is important to note that despite statements of commitment to diversity and inclusivity, demands for social justice concerns to be addressed have continued. This further illustrates that the current discourse on diversity and inclusivity has limitations for social justice.

Leaders in this study acknowledged social difference markers such as race and gender, however, not all the leaders shared reflections on their positions of power and privilege. The racialized leaders in this study reflected on the role their racial identities play in their leadership practice including the tensions that arise when leading for social justice. Tensions in practice arise when there is a pursuit of inclusivity efforts that challenge or unsettle the dominant discourse. Indigenizing the science curriculum at John Thomas' institution is an example of these tensions, yet leaders at the institution have declared a commitment to diversity and inclusivity. Marlen, a self-identified racialized leader in this study, described the tensions that arose when she challenged workshop participants to engage in self-reflexivity on issues of power and privilege. Workshop participants felt that Marlen had labelled them as all racist. She was perceived as the angry woman of color. When leaders engage diversity and inclusivity in ways that do not challenge institutional whiteness, then claims to commitment to these values are limited in that leaders do not engage the realities of institutional inequality (Ahmed, 2012). Furthermore, the limited commitment to values of diversity and inclusion means that inequities in the systemic dimension of praxis in educational contexts persist. It means that the power structures that allow for the dominance of white Eurocentrism in education remain intact.

Some leaders in this study called for an organizational structure that extends beyond conventional discourses of diversity and inclusivity and is reflective of the student demographic for social justice and equity concerns to be addressed. As argued by Kitossa et. al (2020), a critical mass of racialized leaders is required for power inequities in educational systems to be addressed. Having a critical mass in representational diversity must include what Dei (2014) describes as the "politics of claiming space" (p. 246). There is a need for leaders from historically marginalized groups to "pursue a radical politics that transforms our institutions by using our [leaders from historically marginalized groups] presence to intervene, disrupt, and implement alternatives" (p. 246). I argue that while representational diversity is important, simply having representational diversity is insufficient as there is need to disrupt educational leadership that is currently grounded in white Eurocentric ways of knowing (Lopez, 2021). Such a disruption calls for the decolonization of postsecondary leadership. Decolonization is the process of dismantling the structures that uphold and maintain the power and dominance of a particular way of knowing and being over others. In education, decolonization means "removing the vestiges of colonialism from all aspects of schooling and education" (Lopez, 2021, p. 17)

Through the integrated social justice leadership framework for diversity and inclusivity, leaders ought to engage in self-reflexivity and action in relation to colonial knowledge systems, white Eurocentric ways of knowing, power, representation and implicit bias within the dimensions of leadership praxis. Self-reflexivity begins in the personal dimension where leaders need to engage in critical self-reflection on their ways of knowing social justice issues. Additionally, in engaging self-reflexivity on social justice issues, leaders need to question their leadership practices in the personal and interpersonal dimensions in relation to social justice issues in educational contexts. Postsecondary leaders need to answer questions such as: What do postsecondary leaders know and what will they do about the relationship between diversity and inclusivity in relation to white Eurocentric ways of knowing and colonial knowledge systems? With the current decrease in funding to postsecondary institutions and simultaneous pressure on leaders to generate alternate sources of revenue, how can leaders navigate the current demands on themselves for increased efficiency and revenue generation with the calls for social justice concerns to be addressed specifically through questions of equity and decolonization? Equity refers to the "fair, inclusive and respectful treatment of all people, with consideration of individual and group diversities and intersectionality of multiple social identities, access to privileges and impacts of oppression" (The Toronto District School Board, 2014, as cited in Lopez & Olan, 2019, p. 23). Equity in education implies the recognition of socio-cultural power imbalances that privilege some and not others.

Additional questions that postsecondary leaders need to consider are: What do postsecondary leaders understand power, representation, and implicit bias in their leadership praxis to mean in relation to diversity and inclusivity? How might this understanding differ in the context of equity? In what ways can postsecondary leaders enact critical leadership approaches in the various dimensions of praxis in order to address social justice issues? How do postsecondary leaders attend to equity, decolonization and anti-racism in areas such as curriculum, recruitment and hiring? Such engagement would enable leaders to account for how they "come to appreciate and interrogate established hegemonic ways of knowing" (Dei, 2000, p. 25), thus extending the current discourse on diversity and inclusivity in ways that tend to equity and decolonial thought and potentially translate to leadership practices that restore and promote capacity in education.

Lopez (2021) proposed that educational leaders engage the Restoring and Promoting Capacity framework to challenge colonialism in educational leadership. In this framework, decolonizing education is a process that calls for restoring capacity for those whose knowledge and ways of knowing has been erased through colonialism. Restoring capacity in this context means engaging a "collaborative process that is respectful and inclusive grounded in decolonizing philosophies and practice" (p. 56). It is a framework that also calls for promoting capacity in all educators seeking to challenge the vestiges of colonialism. What resonates with me the most in the Restoring and Promoting Capacities framework is the recognition that leaders bring knowledge with them. It is a model that does not approach leadership from a deficit perspective. This approach ties in well with the ways of knowing as described in the integrated social justice leadership framework for diversity and inclusivity. Educational leaders bring with them their ways of knowing and understanding social justice issues.

Assumptions Revisited

In Chapter 1, I identified four assumptions that I held at the beginning of my research. The first assumption was that leadership impacts educational outcomes (Lopez, 2017a; 2017b; Walker & Riordan, 2010). The second assumption was that diversity in leadership benefits higher education in that learning becomes more accessible and that teaching methods become more inclusive of diverse learner needs (Lopez, 2016; Walker & Riordan, 2010; Wolfe & Dilworth, 2015). The third assumption was that leaders help shape meaning and the culture of their organizations (Northouse, 2016; Zembylas & Iasonos, 2010). Finally, there was the assumption that the culture in which leaders lead influences their leadership practices (Burke, 2013; Dimmock & Walker, 2005). In this section, I revisit my initial assumptions in the context of my research findings, interpretation, conclusions and discursive limitations of diversity and inclusivity. Though I still uphold the initial four assumptions, I came to realize during my study that there were additional assumptions I had made, perhaps subconsciously, but had not articulated.

Participants spoke to the importance of representational diversity on educational outcomes. Representational diversity influences the systemic dimension of leadership practice, particularly in relation to the curriculum, learning outcomes, and student life experiences on campus. Leaders draw on personal sociohistorical experiences and their ways of knowing diversity and inclusivity. This influences the decisions they make regarding the curriculum and the services students need to access on campus. My study shows that lack of representational diversity in key decision-making positions negatively impacts curriculum development initiatives, such as Indigenizing the science curriculum.

The assumptions that leaders help shape meaning and the culture of their organizations and that the culture in which leaders lead influences their leadership practices were upheld in this study. Leaders draw on personal sociohistorical experiences and ways of knowing that influence the culture of their institutions. Even where dissonance exists between a leader's way of knowing and orientation to diversity and inclusivity, the actions that the leader takes in the various dimensions of practice help shape meaning. Some leaders create professional development opportunities within the institution such as anti-racist workshops to attend to the issues of social justice. A lack of representational diversity in leadership contributes to maintaining the homogeneous and dominant culture of postsecondary institutions. This impacts the sense of belonging for some racialized leaders. The culture reflected in the institution is of the dominant group. Institutional strategic plans play an important role for leaders in shaping the meaning and culture of their institutions. These plans reflect the culture in which leaders operate. When leaders do not engage critical leadership in the various dimensions of praxis, the white Eurocentric dominant culture remains intact as diversity and inclusivity serve as simply statements.

As I reflected on my research findings through the integrated social justice leadership framework for diversity and inclusivity, I realized that I had an additional assumption that I had not articulated prior to engaging participants. I had initially approached the study with a conceptualization of leadership as "a process whereby an individual influences a group of individuals to achieve a common goal" (Northouse, 2016, p. 6). The process leaders engage, the way in which they evaluate individuals, and the common goals they define are conceptualized using a dominant Eurocentric lens:

> Conceptions of leadership are mired in liberal and neo-liberal agendas that assert ideas of quality, competencies, standards, accountability, and transparency without any critical engagement with equity, social justice, and diverse local and cultural knowings about leadership from the perspective of marginalized and oppressed communities. (Dei, 2019, p. 353)

Eurocentric ways of knowing continue to dominate education and educational leadership. Lopez (2021) argued that current educational leadership practices continue to be sites of colonial oppression where power and control of knowledge, policies, and structures continue to be dominated by Western Eurocentric epistemologies. Now, with the increased diversity in the student demographic in Canadian postsecondary institutions and the increased calls for postsecondary leaders to address social injustices including racism in educational settings, there is a need to critically analyze current leadership approaches through a decolonization lens. Some leaders in my study alluded to different conceptualizations of leadership that were informed by their personal sociohistorical experiences and ways of knowing. However, it appears that most leaders in this study assumed, like I did, a conceptualization of leadership that is steeped in the dominant view. This is a limitation of the current discourse on diversity and inclusivity.

I concur with Lopez (2021) who argued that disrupting educational leadership in ways that attend to social justice concerns requires the decolonization of leadership practices in education. In my interactions with leaders in this study, it became clear that some leaders engage diversity and inclusivity without challenging Eurocentric systems of knowledge, decolonization, colonial ways of knowing and questions of racism. These leaders did not question historical forms of oppression nor the colonial context of education. They were comfortable with the discourse on diversity and inclusivity in their institutions.

The current comfortable discourse on diversity and inclusivity allows for the continued underrepresentation of historically marginalized people in senior leadership positions. It also allows for the continuation of inequities in curricula and learning experiences of BIPOC students. Issues such as racism remain unaddressed. It is not surprising therefore, that diversity and inclusion statements are referenced when concerns of racism and oppression in education are raised. A disruption of current practices calls for current and future leaders to challenge the present discourse on diversity and inclusivity by engaging historical and contemporary discussions concerning equity, decolonization, historical forms of oppression, power and knowledge and implications for postsecondary education.

Conclusion

The current discourse on diversity and inclusivity has limitations in that institutional structures of power, inequity, coloniality, racism, white Eurocentric ways of knowing among more are left intact. For the teaching and learning needs of equity seeking groups to be met and for social justice issues to be addressed, it is important that leaders engage in self-reflexivity that attends to questions of power, equity, and decolonial thought. The integrated social justice leadership framework for diversity and inclusivity provides a way for leaders to understand themselves, their practices and their institutions in ways that can restore and promote capacity to attend to social justice matters.

References

Ahmed, S. (2012). *On being included: Racism and diversity in institutional life*. Duke University Press.

Dei, G. (2000). Towards an Anti-racism discursive framework. In G. S. Dei & A. Calliste (Eds.), *Power, knowledge and anti-racist education* (pp. 23–40). Fernwood Publishing.

Dei, G. J. (2014). Personal reflections on anti-racism education for a global context. *Encounters on Education*, 15, 239–249.

Dei, G. J. S. (2019). An Indigenous Africentric perspective on Black leadership. In T. Kitossa, E. S. Lason, & P. S. S. Howard (Eds.), *African Canadian leadership* (pp. 345–369). University of Toronto Press. https://doi.org/10.3138/9781487531409

Dimmock, C., & Walker, A. (2005). *Educational leadership culture and diversity*. Sage Publications.

James, C. E. (2011b, December 2). Isn't it about time we admit race matters? *EdCan Network*. https://www.edcan.ca/articles/isnt-it-about-time-we-admit-that-race-matters/

Kitossa, T., Blackfoot, A., Costen, W., Campbell, K., & Smith, M. (2020, October 2). *Inclusive decision making structures* [Panel discussion]. National Dialogues and Action for Inclusive Higher Education and Communities, University of Toronto, Canada.

Lopez, A. E. (2017a). Is it time for a sixth dimension of multicultural education?: Resistance and praxis in challenging times. *Multicultural Perspectives, 19*(3), 155–161. https://doi.org/10.1080/15210960.2017.1331740

Lopez, A. E. (2017b). Rocky boats and rainbows: Culturally responsive leadership from the margin – An autoethnography. In A. Esmail, A. Pitre, & A. Aragon (Eds.), *Perspectives on diversity, equity, and social justice in educational leadership* (pp. 23–40). Rowman & Littlefield.

Lopez. A. E. (2021). Examining alternative school leadership practices and approaches: A decolonising school leadership approach. *Intercultural Education*. https://doi.org/10.1080/14675986.2021.1889471

Lopez, A. E., & Olan, E. L. (2019). *Transformative pedagogies for teacher education: Critical action, agency, and dialogue in teaching and learning contexts*. Information Age Publishing.

Northouse, P. (2016). *Leadership: Theory and practice*. Sage Publications.

Walker, A., & Riordan, G. (2010). Leading collective capacity in culturally diverse schools. *School Leadership & Management, 30*(1), 51–63. https://doi.org/10.1080/13632430903509766

Wolfe, B. L., & Dilworth, P. (2015). Transitioning normalcy: Organizational culture, African American administrators, and diversity leadership in higher education. *Review of Educational Research, 85*(4), 667–697. https://doi.org/10.3102/0034654314565667

Zembylas, M., & Iasonos, S. (2010). Leadership styles and multicultural education approaches: An exploration of their relationship. *International Journal of Leadership in Education, 13*(2), 163–183. https://doi.org/10.1080/13603120903386969

· 8 ·

CONCLUSION: POSITIONING LEADERS IN WAYS THAT ATTEND TO EQUITY AND SOCIAL JUSTICE MATTERS

Introduction

In this chapter I share how the phenomenon, diversity and inclusivity, was taken up in my study and what it means for postsecondary leaders in the current educational settings. I discuss this through the integrated social justice leadership framework for diversity and inclusivity, which I developed from knowledge gained through the literature and knowledge generated through my interactions with the leaders in the study. My research led to the development of the framework. Following this, I share my conclusions and discuss the implications and recommendations for leaders in postsecondary settings. I also discuss recommendations for further research. Lastly, I conclude with final reflections on the significance of my research study and the hope for further work to be done in this field.

Integrated Social Justice Leadership Framework for Diversity and Inclusivity

The integrated social justice leadership framework for diversity and inclusivity provides a way to think through how postsecondary leaders make meaning of diversity and inclusivity within the varying dimensions in which they practice leadership in relation to social justice issues in educational settings. The framework provides a way for leaders to consider how they understand themselves, their leadership practice, and the context in which they lead as it relates to diversity and inclusivity. With this understanding, leaders can position their leadership practices in ways that attend to social justice matters. Underpinning the integrated social justice leadership framework for diversity and inclusivity are the praxis-dimensions-capacities framework for social justice leadership (Furman, 2012), ways of knowing in adulthood (Drago-Severson & Blum-DeStefano, 2017), framework for educational inclusivity (DeLuca, 2013), and the work of Canadian critical race and social justice scholars Malinda Smith, Carl E. James, George Sefa Dei, Anne Lopez, and Verna St. Denis, as well as British-Australian scholar Sara Ahmed.

The first finding from my research was that to make meaning of diversity and inclusivity, postsecondary leaders draw on personal sociohistorical experiences. In thinking through the integrated social justice leadership framework for diversity and inclusivity, my understanding is that there are different epistemologies of diversity and inclusivity. This finding is supported by the literature. These epistemologies are informed by personal sociohistorical experiences and ways of knowing or orientation to diversity and inclusivity. A leader's epistemology on diversity and inclusivity influences leadership practice in various domains. Therefore, how leaders orient to diversity and inclusivity is important for understanding the expectations and actions of leaders in the various dimensions of social justice leadership practice.

The second finding from my study was that leaders navigate implicit bias in the personal, communal, interpersonal, and systemic dimensions of praxis. Challenges or tensions arise in these dimensions when there is dissonance among the leaders' different ways of knowing or orientation to diversity and inclusivity as they carry out their leadership tasks. Furthermore, not all the leaders' different ways of knowing and historical experiences synchronize with the various social justice issues in educational settings. This presents a challenge for the implementation of social justice leadership practices and equity. Although the interdisciplinary framework for educational inclusivity (DeLuca, 2013) attempts to address diversity and inclusivity issues for all historically marginalized groups, it does not explicitly address the challenge of "neutrality," the metaphorical "brick wall," colonial knowledge systems, white Eurocentric ways of knowing, or the implicit bias that historically marginalized people face in organizations. The notion of the concentric power circles proposed in the educational inclusivity framework, where all diverse groups are deemed equal contributors, do not seem to attend to the complex intersecting identities of individuals and the accompanying varying power differentials that may exist. Identifying and naming colonial knowledge systems and white Eurocentric ways of knowing simultaneously recognizing and understanding intersecting identities and power relationships in the various dimensions is key to navigating implicit bias. I therefore conclude that how leaders navigate the challenges of implicit bias in the various dimensions of social justice praxis is informed by their ways of knowing, sociopolitical and critical consciousness, understanding of coloniality, power relations and intersecting identities in historically marginalized populations.

The third finding from my study was that leaders engage their institution's strategic direction on diversity and inclusivity. Institutions provide a frame for praxis (reflection and action) in the various dimensions in the form of strategic plans and support for transformational leadership. However, it appears that the strategic plans and transformational leadership practices do not include a critical perspective or consciousness that takes up social justice issues in a way that seeks structural and systemic change. The issues brought forward by the Scholar Strike and Students4Change, for example, point to a need to address systemic racism in educational institutions. The strategic plans shared by participants are presented from a position of neutrality where diversity is welcomed and celebrated. I conclude, therefore, that although strategic plans are important, they are presented as "neutral" and do not question what is already in place which is colonial knowledge systems and white Eurocentric ways of knowing. Attending to social justice issues necessitates addressing questions of power and dominance in the systemic dimension, particularly in postsecondary institutions where leaders have declared commitments to diversity and inclusivity.

The fourth finding from my study was that leaders encounter issues of representational diversity. I advance representational diversity in this study as including racialized people. There is dissonance for some leaders, particularly those who appear to have self-authoring and self-transforming ways of knowing, with respect to representational diversity in the various dimensions of practice in their institutions. These leaders appear to come up against the metaphorical "brick wall" and find that there are no other leaders that look like them or approach diversity and inclusivity from a critical perspective like they do; they question their worthiness in their leadership positions. I therefore conclude that a lack of representational diversity negatively impacts the sense of belonging of racialized leaders. Representational diversity in leaders, or lack thereof, influences the systemic dimension in educational institutions, particularly in curriculum development, hiring, and recruitment. Therefore, a lack of representational diversity at the senior leadership level means that historically marginalized voices and perspectives are not in the radar of institution-wide decision-making discussions and positions that impact educational outcomes. They are not in power and are not represented in key structural positions.

Furthermore, leaders encounter issues of representational diversity that are in part due to immigration patterns and trends in the society at large. These immigration patterns play a role in the student demographic and the make-up of the candidate pool of individuals responding to recruitment calls for teaching positions. I also conclude that for social justice issues to be addressed, it is important that leaders understand the influence of the sociopolitical context as it relates to representational diversity in teaching, learning, and the recruitment of teaching faculty.

Lastly, the fifth finding from my study was that leaders situate diversity and inclusivity issues in the provincial sociopolitical context. Some leaders in this study described what they perceived to be a misalignment between the diversity and inclusivity values of their institutions and provincial discussions of diversity and inclusivity matters by politicians. From their perspectives, their institutions supported diversity and inclusivity values, even though for some leaders there was a misalignment between their personal sociohistorical experiences and the positioning of the institution. From the perspective of these leaders, the position of the newly elected provincial government did not appear to be supportive of diversity and inclusivity. I argued in Chapter 5 of this study that there are similarities between the institutional structures, culture, and orientation toward diversity and inclusivity and the provincial sociopolitical positioning on these concepts. Furthermore, critical leadership approaches that are non-Western and nonheteronormative are not reflected in the current provincial sociopolitical context or in the postsecondary institutional organizational culture. Therefore, I conclude that the organizational culture of postsecondary institutions and the collective orientation toward diversity and inclusivity is reflective of the provincial sociopolitical positioning on diversity and inclusivity.

Implications and Recommendations for Postsecondary Leaders with a View to Equity

Scholars have proposed several frameworks that attend to the complex phenomenon of diversity and inclusivity. Some scholars have made efforts to address the complexity of diversity and inclusivity through integrative and interdisciplinary approaches (Dei, 2000; DeLuca, 2013). My research shows that to understand how postsecondary leaders make meaning of diversity and inclusivity in the current complex context, there is a need for a more holistic framework through which leaders can engage when considering leadership practice that attends to the needs of the student demographic and evolving campus culture. The integrated social justice leadership framework for diversity and inclusivity provides a way for leaders to think through their and others' understanding of diversity and inclusivity within the varying dimensions in which they practice leadership in postsecondary settings. With this understanding, leaders can engage leadership practices in ways that attend to equity and social justice matters. In this section I draw upon the integrated social justice leadership framework for diversity and inclusivity to discuss implications and recommendations for postsecondary leaders with a view to restoring and promoting capacity (Lopez, 2021) to achieve equity in educational contexts. Figure 8.1 is a visual representation of how leaders can engage the integrated social justice leadership framework for diversity and inclusivity to restore and promote capacity in attending to equity and social justice concerns in educational contexts.

Self-reflexivity in Relation to social justice for equity

Critical Leadership Approaches

Restoring & Promoting Capacity

Figure 8.1. Integrated Social Justice Leadership Framework for Diversity and Inclusivity with a view to Equity
Source: Maroro Zinyemba

I concluded that how leaders orient to diversity and inclusivity is important for understanding the expectations and actions of leaders in the various dimensions of social justice leadership practice. I also concluded that how leaders navigate the challenges of implicit bias in the various dimensions of praxis is informed by their ways of knowing and understanding of colonial knowledge systems, white Eurocentric ways of knowing, power relations and the intersecting identities of historically marginalized populations. These conclusions mean that, as leaders engage in leadership practice, thought should be given to their sociopolitical and critical consciousness, own ways of knowing diversity and inclusivity, and how these ways address the social justice issues that historically marginalized people are calling attention to in educational settings. I recommend that leaders engage in self-reflexivity to name and identify coloniality and white Eurocentric ways of knowing in postsecondary contexts. This self-reflexivity begins in the personal dimension of praxis and should extend to the interpersonal, communal, systemic and ecological dimensions. Leaders need to articulate a plan for critical self-reflexivity to address power relations, inequity in education and multiple intersecting identities through a decolonization lens in relation to and along with various marginalized populations. Such a plan positions leaders for further exploration of their ways of knowing and action in relation to equity and social justice matters. Additionally, such a plan sets the foundation to restore and promote capacity in leaders to attend to social justice concerns in all the dimensions of praxis.

The third conclusion in my study is that strategic plans are important, as they articulate the position of institutions on diversity and inclusivity and leaders actively engage these plans, but they are presented as "neutral" and do not critically question what is already in place. Questions of power and dominance in the system are not addressed through this discourse of diversity and inclusivity. This means that, as leaders engage in practice, a critical look needs to be cast on strategic plans and ensuing actions as they relate to the calls to attend to social justice issues and equity. I recommend that leaders clearly articulate how social justice issues of colonial knowledge systems, white Eurocentric ways of knowing, power, representation, implicit bias and achieving equity are addressed in the strategic plans.

Representational diversity in leadership is a key factor in matters involving diversity and inclusivity. I reached two conclusions related to representational diversity in leadership in my study: a lack of representational diversity in leadership has a bearing upon the sense of belonging of racialized leaders and a lack of representational diversity at the senior leadership level means that historically marginalized voices and perspectives are not included in institution-wide decision-making discussions and positions that impact educational outcomes. These conclusions point to the need for leaders to critically reflect on the leadership approaches they engage and consider how historically marginalized voices are represented or not represented in important decision-making positions and processes and the role of strategic plans to consider equity, anti-racism and decolonial thought.

Though transformational and adaptive leadership approaches relate to change in values and beliefs and have been broached in relation to diversity and inclusivity, these approaches are limited in that they are silent on matters of equity, anti-racism, dominance and power structures. There is a need for representational diversity in senior leadership positions to help shape a more inclusive institutional culture. I also concluded that it is important for leaders to understand the influence of the sociopolitical context as it relates to representational diversity in teaching, learning, and the recruitment of teaching faculty.

Some of the leaders who participated in my study reflected on and situated diversity and inclusivity matters in the larger sociopolitical context or ecological dimension. I recommend that all leaders consider and articulate barriers that historically marginalized students, teaching faculty, and postsecondary leaders face using a decolonizing and antiracism lens, not only in the systemic dimension, but in the larger sociopolitical or ecological dimension also. I concluded that the organizational culture of postsecondary institutions and the collective orientation toward diversity and inclusivity is reflective of the provincial sociopolitical discussion by politicians on diversity and inclusivity. This means that different critical leadership approaches, particularly those that are not of the dominant view, such as decolonizing, antiracism, and Indigenous leadership approaches, could be challenging to engage given the sociopolitical climate in which leaders operate. Despite this challenge, it would be valuable for leaders to explore different critical leadership approaches as opportunities for greater understanding of social justice leadership and positioning leadership practices and the institutions they lead in ways that restore and promote capacity to address equity and social justice matters.

Recommendations for Further Research

In developing the integrated social justice leadership framework for diversity and inclusivity, I hope that my research has contributed to a more holistic and deeper understanding of how postsecondary leaders make meaning of diversity and inclusivity in educational settings. Upon reflecting on the findings of my study and the ensuing discussion, I have contemplated additional areas for further research that may further deepen the understanding of the phenomenon of diversity and inclusivity, and position leadership practice in postsecondary contexts in ways that address equity and social justice matters effectively.

Drago-Severson and Blum-DeStefano (2017) posited four ways of knowing in adulthood in relation to diversity and social justice leadership, which are instrumental, socializing, self-authoring, and self-transforming. Their framework connects the ways of knowing to teaching and leading for social justice. Furman (2012) proposed the dimensions of social justice leadership praxis (personal, interpersonal, communal, systemic, and ecological) to gain a deeper and more holistic understanding of the nature of social justice leadership in order to inform leadership preparation programs (p. 213). My study provided insights into how leaders understand themselves, their leadership practice in the various dimensions, and the context in which they lead as it relates to diversity and inclusivity. It would be valuable to conduct a study where leaders explore their unique ways of knowing in relation to social justice issues as framed by colonial knowledge systems, white Eurocentric ways of knowing, power, representation, and implicit bias, and how these issues inform their leadership practice in each of the different dimensions of praxis. Further, it would be valuable to research ways in which leaders can engage their unique ways of knowing to critically analyze through a decolonization lens their own leadership practices in the various dimensions of praxis. This would help build knowledge of what Furman stated is a need for a more holistic understanding of the nature of social justice leadership. This knowledge could inform decision-making at senior leadership levels, the development of institutional strategic plans, and the design of leadership preparation programs, professional development, or learning opportunities for leaders.

I described in Chapter 7 that in thinking through the integrated social justice leadership framework for diversity and inclusivity, I realized that leaders in my study were largely silent on different critical leadership approaches, such as Indigenous leadership. There is a research opportunity to explore social justice leadership praxis from the perspectives of leaders from historically marginalized communities. Such research could take up a different methodology such as multiple case study. This research would deepen our understanding of the phenomenon from various perspectives and could inform different ways of enacting social justice leadership practice in order to attend to equity issues and the educational needs of all students in postsecondary institutions.

A final recommendation for further research would be to engage the integrated social justice leadership framework for diversity and inclusivity to explore the perspectives of postsecondary presidents, vice presidents, and members of the Board of Governors of postsecondary institutions in Alberta on diversity and inclusivity in postsecondary leadership and how these perspectives can translate to action plans that address equity and social justice issues. The Board of Governors is influential in that it is responsible for creating institutional policy and has senior oversight of the institution. According to the Alberta Advanced Education (2017) *Guidelines for Board of Governors Members*, some responsibilities of the Board of Governors that are related to my research include appointing the president of the institution and monitoring their performance, approving the institution's plans and policies, and maintaining government relations and accountability (p. 18). The Board of Governors has influence in the various dimensions of leadership praxis, particularly the systemic and ecological dimensions. Gaining an understanding of how members of the Board of Governors make meaning of diversity and inclusivity in postsecondary educational settings and how this can translate to action would shed light on the institutional strategic direction, position on diversity and inclusivity, and actions that need to be taken to attend to matters of equity and social justice. Engaging the Board of Governors, presidents and vice presidents through the integrated social justice leadership framework for diversity and inclusivity could position postsecondary institutions in ways that effectively address social justice matters.

Final Reflections

I have been a member of the stage platform at several convocation ceremonies at my institution. As a postsecondary leader, I have the honour and privilege of sitting on the stage and witnessing graduands complete a leg of their educational journey. It is always an emotional experience for me. There is the excitement, the sense of accomplishment, and the satisfaction that I feel as an educational leader. However, I am also always acutely aware of how visible I am on that stage given that I have often been the only black person there, yet year after year many black graduands walk across the stage. I always wondered how this came to be. The diversity in the student population is certainly not reflected in the senior leadership of the institution. Inevitably, after almost every convocation ceremony, a black person from the audience comes up to me as I congratulate graduands in the foyer and states in one way or another how happy they are to see themselves represented through me as part of the stage platform party. It is bittersweet.

I came to my research with a desire to gain a deeper understanding of what diversity and inclusivity mean to postsecondary leaders. It seemed to me that how I understood the phenomenon was different from my colleagues. I came with questions on the practices leaders engaged regarding diversity and inclusivity. I came to my study with the knowledge that several Canadian scholars had been researching this topic for some time. Scholars such as Malinda Smith, Carl E. James, Enakshi Dua among many more have proven through their research and work that equity in Canadian universities does not exist despite decades of equity policies and legal requirements. The same can be said of Canadian colleges. I wondered why. I learned through the conversations with leaders in my study that they approached diversity and inclusivity in different ways and that they engaged leadership practice in different and multiple spheres. During my study, the Black Lives Matter movement regained momentum as a result of the death of George Floyd at the hands of law enforcement in the United States of America. This had ripple effects as several institutions, including my own, reiterated their commitments to diversity and inclusivity. In the postsecondary context, there followed several national dialogues and lectures on racism in the academy and discussions on what needs to be done. This confirmed for me that my research was timely. I was able to include what I had learned through these national dialogues in my study.

I realized that it was important for me to interpret my interactions with the leaders holistically and not be limited to one framework. Articulating the interpretation of my findings through the integrated social justice leadership framework for diversity and inclusivity was an illuminative experience for me. I learned that my own conceptualization of leadership was steeped in colonial knowledge systems and that as a leader I need to re-engage decolonial thought through self-reflexivity and practice. It is my hope that the integrated social justice leadership framework for inclusivity has contributed to knowledge on leadership, diversity, and inclusivity in educational organizations and that it will be useful for further research by other scholars and for positioning leaders to restore and promote capacity for equity in educational contexts. At a personal level, the framework has helped me make sense of my reality as a leader working in an institution that has publicly declared a commitment to diversity and inclusivity. The framework presents a useful platform for leaders to cocreate new knowledge and experiences that will help restore and promote capacity in the quest for equity in educational contexts.

As I conclude, I feel in many ways that my journey has only just begun. There is more research that needs to be done in order to meet the needs of students from all backgrounds, including students from historically marginalized communities. There is need to apply the integrated social justice leadership framework for diversity and inclusivity to attend to matters of anti-racism and decolonization in education.

The purpose of my research was to understand how postsecondary leaders in Alberta make meaning of diversity and inclusivity in educational settings. I engaged a qualitative case study methodology where I interacted with nine postsecondary leaders in Alberta. Knowledge gained from in-depth interactions with the leaders and from the literature I studied contributed to the development of the integrated social justice leadership framework for diversity and inclusivity. This framework signals the importance of leaders understanding themselves, their leadership practice, and the context in which they lead in order for them to position themselves and the institutions they lead in ways that address equity and social justice matters.

References

Alberta Advanced Education. (2017). Guidelines for board of governors members: An introduction to board governance at Alberta's public post-secondary institutions. https://open.alberta.ca/publications/guidelines-for-board-of-governors-members

Dei, G. (2000). Towards an Anti-racism discursive framework. In G. S. Dei & A. Calliste (Eds.), *Power, knowledge and anti-racist education* (pp. 23–40). Fernwood Publishing.

DeLuca, C. (2013). Toward an interdisciplinary framework for educational inclusivity. *Canadian Journal of Education*, 36(1), 305–348.

Drago-Severson, E., & Blum-DeStefano, J. (2017). The self in social justice: A developmental lens on race, identity, and transformation. *Harvard Educational Review*, 87(4), 457–481.

Furman, G. (2012). Social justice leadership as praxis: Developing capacities through preparation programs. *Educational Administration Quarterly*, 48(2), 191–229. https://doi.org/10.1177/0013161X11427394

Henry, F., Dua, E., James, C. E., Kobayashi, A., Li, P., Ramos, H., & Smith, M. S. (Eds.). (2017). *The equity myth: Racialization and indigeneity at Canadian universities*. University of British Columbia Press.

Lopez. A. E. (2021). Examining alternative school leadership practices and approaches: A decolonising school leadership approach. *Intercultural Education*. https://doi.org/10.1080/14675986.2021.1889471

INDEX

Studies in Criticality

General Editor
Shirley R. Steinberg

Counterpoints publishes the most compelling and imaginative books being written in education today. Grounded on the theoretical advances in criticalism, feminism, and postmodernism in the last two decades of the twentieth century, Counterpoints engages the meaning of these innovations in various forms of educational expression. Committed to the proposition that theoretical literature should be accessible to a variety of audiences, the series insists that its authors avoid esoteric and jargonistic languages that transform educational scholarship into an elite discourse for the initiated. Scholarly work matters only to the degree it affects consciousness and practice at multiple sites. Counterpoints' editorial policy is based on these principles and the ability of scholars to break new ground, to open new conversations, to go where educators have never gone before.

For additional information about this series or for the submission of manuscripts, please contact:

Shirley R. Steinberg, General Editor
msgramsci@gmail.com

To order other books in this series, please contact our Customer Service Department:

peterlang@presswarehouse.com (within the U.S.)
orders@peterlang.com (outside the U.S.)

Or browse online by series:

www.peterlang.com